I0009858

Raspberry Pi Mechatronics Projects HOTSH⊕T

Enter the world of mechatronic systems with the Raspberry Pi to design and build 12 amazing projects

Sai Yamanoor

Srihari Yamanoor

PUBLISHING

BIRMINGHAM - MUMBAI

Raspberry Pi Mechatronics Projects HOTSHOT

Copyright © 2015 Packt Publishing

All rights reserved. No part of this book may be reproduced, stored in a retrieval system, or transmitted in any form or by any means, without the prior written permission of the publisher, except in the case of brief quotations embedded in critical articles or reviews.

Every effort has been made in the preparation of this book to ensure the accuracy of the information presented. However, the information contained in this book is sold without warranty, either express or implied. Neither the authors, nor Packt Publishing, and its dealers and distributors will be held liable for any damages caused or alleged to be caused directly or indirectly by this book.

Packt Publishing has endeavored to provide trademark information about all of the companies and products mentioned in this book by the appropriate use of capitals. However, Packt Publishing cannot guarantee the accuracy of this information.

First published: February 2015

Production reference: 1190215

Published by Packt Publishing Ltd.
Livery Place
35 Livery Street
Birmingham B3 2PB, UK.

ISBN 978-1-84969-622-7

www.packtpub.com

Credits

Authors

Sai Yamanoor

Srihari Yamanoor

Reviewers

Guy Scheffer

Sreedhar Vaddi

Cheuk Yu

Commissioning Editor

Usha Iyer

Acquisition Editors

Usha Iyer

Rebecca Pedley

Sam Wood

Content Development Editor

Susmita Sabot

Technical Editor

Parag Topre

Copy Editor

Janbal Dharmaraj

Project Coordinator

Milton D'souza

Proofreaders

Simran Bhogal

Maria Gould

Ameesha Green

Paul Hindle

Indexer

Hemangini Bari

Graphics

Sheetal Aute

Disha Haria

Production Coordinators

Aparna Bhagat

Manu Joseph

Cover Work

Aparna Bhagat

About the Authors

Sai Yamanoor is a mechatronics engineer working for a private start-up school in the San Francisco Bay Area where he builds devices that help students achieve their full potential. He completed his degree in mechanical engineering at Carnegie Mellon University, Pittsburgh, PA, and his undergraduate work in mechatronics at Sri Krishna College of Engineering and Technology, Coimbatore, India. His interests, deeply rooted in DIY and open software and hardware cultures, include developing gadgets and apps that improve quality of life, Internet of Things, crowdfunding, education, and new technologies. In his spare time, he plays with various devices and architectures such as Raspberry Pi, Arduino, Galileo, Android devices, and others. Sai shares his adventures with mechatronics at the aptly named "Mechatronics Craze" blog at `http://mechatronicscraze.wordpress.com/`.

I want to thank my parents for encouraging me in all my endeavors and for making me what I am today. I am grateful to my brother who has helped shape my career all these years. I look forward to working with Srihari on similar projects in the future. I sincerely thank Mr. S. Balaji Raghavendra who has been a great source of inspiration to me while pursuing my undergraduate degree. I am also thankful to Susmita Sabot and the entire support team at Packt Publishing who were patient and understood the circumstances during difficult times.

Srihari Yamanoor is a nature photographer and mechanical engineer with experience working in medical device design and CAD/CAM. He completed his master's in science as well as a degree in engineering from Stanford University. His work and interests in medical devices include women's health, cancer, orthopedics, and cardiovascular diseases, as well as newer areas such as digital health and electronic health records. He has several thousands of hours of CAD experience behind him and is also certified among other things as a SolidWorks expert, simulation professional, and a SolidWorks instructor. His interests range from engineering and education to social entrepreneurship, animal welfare, and crowdfunding.

I would like to thank my parents, Narasimhan and Yasoda Venakatakrishnan, for their steadfast support in my education and efforts throughout the years, culminating in projects such as this book. Over the course of the years, many friends have helped both Sai and me grow in many ways. For this reason, I would like to say a big word of thanks, in no particular order, to Rika Catherine Hirachi, Anna Liu Jao, Shirupa Gupta, Patrick Nguyen, Vishnu Prasad Ramachandran, Andrew Eib, Christopher Ma, and Karthik Palaniappan. I am sure I am missing some names, and for this, I apologize in advance. I would also like to thank my gracious mentors, Dr. Kevin Waldron, Dr. James Stubbs, Russell Sampson, Mukund Patel, and as I fondly call him, Cyril "Master", all of whom have given me advice and shown me the way. I would like to especially thank my first cat, Squeaky, and the felines Bob, Saxon, and Fishbone, that have followed me, for inspiring me and pushing me to stay on track and keep an eye on the big picture.

About the Reviewers

Sreedhar Vaddi has 4 years of experience in big data, 4 years in cloud computing, and 15 years in Java. His experience includes work in the fields of big data security, biomedical/healthcare, mobile security, financial services (wholesale, mortgage, investment, and brokerage), the Web (marketplace, crowdsourcing, and advertising), news and entertainment, property and casualty insurance, software product development, and scientific research.

He has hands-on experience as an architect working on enterprise mobile applications, Hadoop, SaaS, PaaS, IaaS, the cloud, rich enterprise applications, n-tier enterprise systems, Enterprise Application Integration (EAI) in web-enabling legacy systems, IBM Mainframe and SAP, and SOA web services with Java2 and JEE.

He has also worked in all phases of SDLC, namely designing, developing, performance testing, and implementing Web-2.0, Web-UI, server-side, middleware, and mobile applications. He has also worked with Big 5 Consulting and Fortune 100 companies. He has led teams of sizes varying from 2 to 80 across the globe in different time zones, cultures, and dialects.

He is an administrator of JEE containers (Geronimo, WebSphere, Weblogic, JBoss, and Tomcat) and CDH. He is also a technical consultant at a stealth mode start-up in animal care in the clinical trials industry. He is a diligent worker and quick learner with excellent problem solving, presentation, and mentoring skills.

Cheuk Yu is pursuing a bachelor's degree in electrical engineering at the University of California, Los Angeles (UCLA), with an emphasis on circuit and signal processing. He worked on multiple embedded systems projects using various microcontrollers such as Arduino, Teensy, and Raspberry Pi. As a student researcher for the ELFIN CubeSat Mission at UCLA, he also has hands-on experience working on printed circuit boards, including designing and testing avionics and ground support equipment boards. Besides work and study, he is also an amateur radio operator and astronomer.

www.PacktPub.com

Support files, eBooks, discount offers, and more

For support files and downloads related to your book, please visit www.PacktPub.com.

Did you know that Packt offers eBook versions of every book published, with PDF and ePub files available? You can upgrade to the eBook version at www.PacktPub.com and as a print book customer, you are entitled to a discount on the eBook copy. Get in touch with us at service@packtpub.com for more details.

At www.PacktPub.com, you can also read a collection of free technical articles, sign up for a range of free newsletters and receive exclusive discounts and offers on Packt books and eBooks.

https://www2.packtpub.com/books/subscription/packtlib

Do you need instant solutions to your IT questions? PacktLib is Packt's online digital book library. Here, you can search, access, and read Packt's entire library of books.

Why subscribe?

- ▸ Fully searchable across every book published by Packt
- ▸ Copy and paste, print, and bookmark content
- ▸ On demand and accessible via a web browser

Free access for Packt account holders

If you have an account with Packt at www.PacktPub.com, you can use this to access PacktLib today and view 9 entirely free books. Simply use your login credentials for immediate access.

Table of Contents

Preface

The Raspberry Pi is a quaint example of technological innovations that come by once every two or three decades and set off a revolution that touches every aspect of human life from scientific exploration to entertainment to education. What is exciting this time around is that there are several such innovations happening simultaneously. They might sound like, and are in a way, buzzwords, but they are in fact real, and are changing our lives in so many ways, so few of which we are consciously aware of. We are speaking of innovations in entrepreneurship, such as crowdsourcing or the emergence of DIY with an almost cult-like following to innovations in technology that are current, such as 3D printing and Internet of Everything, and innovations that are impending such as 4D printing, smart manufacturing, and much more.

The Raspberry Pi has already found several uses as evidenced by hundreds of websites, project examples, and crowdsourcing campaigns. People have used the Pi to build robots, teach programming, restore old gaming consoles, stream videos, collect data, and do many other things. The Pi itself has gone through design iterations and continues to spur competing systems. People have taken advantage of this and have hooked up the Pi to many different ecosystems, expanding its ubiquity and utility.

The purpose of this book is to help those who are excited about the Raspberry Pi and have project ideas in mind, or would simply like to get their hands dirty and practice implementing projects so that they can then use that knowledge for other endeavors. We tried to take a practical approach, introducing the Pi in the first couple of project that you can skip if you are familiar with the Raspberry Pi and have used it before. We then discuss projects of increasing complexity. We have also attempted to diversify the projects to demonstrate various uses for the Pi throughout the book.

What this book covers

Project 1, Hello World, will introduce the Raspberry Pi and remind you of things that you should know as you proceed through the book. We will set up the Raspberry Pi and blink an LED.

Project 2, A Raspberry WebIDE Example, will take you through Python development using a browser. We will use the Adafruit WebIDE and lead you through the development process using Adafruit products as props for the examples.

Project 3, The Arduino Raspberry Pi Interface, is inspired by the Harry Potter series, and in an effort to show our love for this series, we have created a clock similar to the innovative and endearing Weasley clock using the Raspberry Pi and an Arduino. This project, of course, allows the clock to report back weather conditions.

Project 4, Christmas Light Sequencer, discusses holidays as the best time for DIY projects, and if you are ever starved of ideas, holidays are the best time to cook up ideas. We picked a Christmas-themed project to demonstrate controlling appliances connected to a local network using Raspberry Pi.

Project 5, Internet of Things Example – An E-mail Alert Water Fountain, follows the theme of the previous project. We will show you how to control a decorative fountain such that anytime you receive a new e-mail, your fountain's light will flash an alert (this can also be switched to receive Twitter alerts).

Project 6, Raspberry Pi as a Personal Assistant, will show you how you can use the Pi as your personal assistant, reminding you of chores, setting alarms, and doing everything at your command.

Project 7, Raspberry Pi-based Line Following Robot, will take you through the simplest of all robots, the line following bot, with Raspberry Pi at the helm. This project will show you the way for this and other complex robotics projects you wish to implement.

Project 8, Connect Four Desktop Game using Raspberry Pi, follows the instant-classic theme for the Raspberry Pi, which includes games. All manners of gaming applications, including the revival of archaic games to new ones and mods, are being created using the Raspberry Pi. We will implement the game using a push button interface.

Project 9, The Raspberry Pi-enabled Pet/Wildlife Monitor, will walk you through a fun example of a bird feeder monitor that allows you to trigger a photo capture each time the bird approaches the feeder. You can think of extending this to other pets, or say, the feral cats in your colony.

Project 10, Raspberry Pi Personal Health Monitor, is a project where we set up a simple web server to record our personal health parameters, build a simple tool to remind ourselves to remain physically active, and remind ourselves to refill a prescription via e-mail alerts.

Project 11, Home Automation using Raspberry Pi, is a project where we will show you how to control appliances using a twisted network where the appliance is connected to a platform such as an Arduino. The Raspberry Pi acts as a server that controls all such nodes in the network.

Project 12, *Using a Raspberry Pi for Science and Education*, is a project packed with examples, including a vocabulary learning tool, a web host for Khan Academy, and a windmill generator science exhibit. Have fun learning and teaching!

Project 13, *Tips and Tricks*, is a project packed with tips and tricks that will help you use the Raspberry Pi!

You can also get the videos, tips and tricks, and many more things related to the projects at `http://diywithpi.com/`.

What you need for this book

To get started, you will need the Raspberry Pi, a monitor, a keyboard, a power source, and preferably, a laptop or personal computer running on any OS—Windows, Linux, or Apple. Other hardware and software recommendations are made in the individual projects, and you are welcome to replace them with what you see fit. A working knowledge of Python is preferred, but not required.

Who this book is for

This book is primarily aimed at hobbyists and do-it-yourself enthusiasts as well as those looking to implement specific projects using low cost hardware and software centered around the Raspberry Pi. Basic exposure to electronics, programming, and Internet usage is assumed. We have tried to take a pragmatic approach, implementing the projects and showing how you can do this on your own.

Conventions

In this book, you will find several headings appearing frequently. To give clear instructions of how to complete a procedure or task, we use:

Mission briefing

This section explains what you will build, with a screenshot of the completed project.

Why is it awesome?

This section explains why the project is cool, unique, exciting, and interesting. It describes what advantage the project will give you.

Your Hotshot objectives

This section explains the eight major tasks required to complete your project.

- ▶ Task 1
- ▶ Task 2
- ▶ Task 3
- ▶ Task 4
- ▶ Task 5
- ▶ Task 6
- ▶ Task 7
- ▶ Task 8

Mission checklist

This section explains any pre-requisites for the project, such as resources or libraries that need to be downloaded, and so on.

Task 1

This section explains the task that you will perform.

Prepare for lift off

This section explains any preliminary work that you may need to do before beginning work on the task.

Engage thrusters

This section lists the steps required in order to complete the task.

Objective complete – mini debriefing

This section explains how the steps performed in the previous section allows us to complete the task. This section is mandatory.

Classified intel

This section provides some extra information relevant to the task.

You will also find a number of styles of text that distinguish between different kinds of information. Here are some examples of these styles, and an explanation of their meaning.

Code words in text, database table names, folder names, filenames, file extensions, pathnames, dummy URLs, user input, and Twitter handles are shown as follows: "We will go through the important features of the pygame module, which is necessary to build our arcade game, including playing sounds and controlling the menu."

A block of code is set as follows:

```
GPIO.output(25, True)
while 1:
    GPIO.output(25,False)
    sleep(1)
    GPIO.output(25,True)
    sleep(1)
```

Any command-line input or output is written as follows:

```
# cp /usr/src/asterisk-addons/configs/cdr_mysql.conf.sample
    /etc/asterisk/cdr_mysql.conf
```

New terms and **important words** are shown in bold. Words that you see on the screen, in menus or dialog boxes for example, appear in the text like this: "clicking the **Next** button moves you to the next screen".

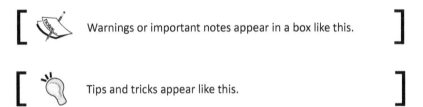

Warnings or important notes appear in a box like this.

Tips and tricks appear like this.

Reader feedback

Feedback from our readers is always welcome. Let us know what you think about this book—what you liked or may have disliked. Reader feedback is important for us to develop titles that you really get the most out of.

To send us general feedback, simply send an e-mail to feedback@packtpub.com, and mention the book title via the subject of your message.

If there is a topic that you have expertise in and you are interested in either writing or contributing to a book, see our author guide on www.packtpub.com/authors.

Customer support

Now that you are the proud owner of a Packt book, we have a number of things to help you to get the most from your purchase.

Downloading the example code

You can download the example code files for all Packt books you have purchased from your account at http://www.packtpub.com. If you purchased this book elsewhere, you can visit http://www.packtpub.com/support and register to have the files e-mailed directly to you.

Downloading the color images of this book

We also provide you a PDF file that has color images of the screenshots/diagrams used in this book. The color images will help you better understand the changes in the output. You can download this file from http://www.packtpub.com/sites/default/files/downloads/6227OT_ColoredImages.pdf.

Errata

Although we have taken every care to ensure the accuracy of our content, mistakes do happen. If you find a mistake in one of our books—maybe a mistake in the text or the code—we would be grateful if you would report this to us. By doing so, you can save other readers from frustration and help us improve subsequent versions of this book. If you find any errata, please report them by visiting http://www.packtpub.com/submit-errata, selecting your book, clicking on the **errata submission form** link, and entering the details of your errata. Once your errata are verified, your submission will be accepted and the errata will be uploaded on our website, or added to any list of existing errata, under the Errata section of that title. Any existing errata can be viewed by selecting your title from http://www.packtpub.com/support.

Piracy

Piracy of copyright material on the Internet is an ongoing problem across all media. At Packt, we take the protection of our copyright and licenses very seriously. If you come across any illegal copies of our works, in any form, on the Internet, please provide us with the location address or website name immediately so that we can pursue a remedy.

Please contact us at copyright@packtpub.com with a link to the suspected pirated material.

We appreciate your help in protecting our authors, and our ability to bring you valuable content.

Questions

You can contact us at questions@packtpub.com if you are having a problem with any aspect of the book, and we will do our best to address it.

Project 1
Hello World

It is a *Hotshot* custom to begin learning anything new with a Hello World example. Since we will be doing really cool things in this book, we will say "Hello World" in a unique fashion. In this project, we will use the Raspberry Pi to cause an LED light to blink. This project is directed towards those who are relatively new to the Raspberry Pi environment as a warm-up exercise. Feel free to skip ahead if you have already done this with your Pi, though we suggest you look through and make sure you haven't missed anything.

A quick introduction to the Raspberry Pi

If we search for the term **Raspberry Pi** over the web or open the Raspberry Pi Foundation's webpage, we will find that the Raspberry Pi is a computer that is the size of a credit card.

Parts of a Raspberry Pi

Features of a Raspberry Pi

The Raspberry Pi Foundation (http://www.raspberrypi.org/) initially released the Raspberry Pi model B. This was followed by the Raspberry Pi model A. In 2014, the Raspberry Pi foundation released variants B+ and A+. The Raspberry Pi models A and A+ (costing 25 USD and 20 USD respectively) do not come with an Ethernet port, a USB port and 256 MB RAM. The model A+ replaced model A while the model B+ replaced model B. The model B (price: 35 USD) came with an Ethernet port, 2 USB ports, and 512 MB RAM; model B+, which supersedes model B, comes with 40 pin GPIO header as opposed to 26 in the earlier models, and has 4 USB ports and a micro SD card slot instead of the SD slot. Per the Raspberry Pi Foundation website, model B+ (as well as model A+) consumes lower power, has better audio and a better form factor, which we certainly concur with. The model A+ also comes with a 40 pin GPIO header and a micro SD card slot. The models A+ and B+ have nine more GPIO pins than their predecessors.

[The Raspberry Pi 2 was released after we finished writing the book. Please refer to the book's site to find out more about getting started with model 2.]

The objective of this book is to build cool projects using the Raspberry Pi. We will discuss the components of Raspberry Pi from this perspective. If you are interested in finding out more about the Raspberry Pi, the Raspberry Pi Foundation's webpage has published the technical specifications of all the components.

First, we will discuss the components available on the Raspberry Pi and the use of these components in our projects. The components of the Raspberry Pi include:

- 2 USB ports (1 USB port available in model A)
- Ethernet port (available only in models B and B+)
- RCA output
- HDMI output
- Audio output
- Low level peripherals, which include:
    - **GPIO (General Purpose Input Output)**
    - **UART/Serial Port (Universal Asynchronous Receiver Transmitter)**
    - **I2C (two wire interface)**
    - **SPI (Serial Peripheral Interface)**

Where can I buy a Raspberry Pi?

Element14 and **RS Components** are the most common distributors of the Raspberry Pi in the United States. The Raspberry Pi model A was roughly priced at 25 USD, while its successor model A+ was priced at 20 USD. The model B was priced at 35 USD and the model B+ is priced at 40 USD. There are also an ever increasing number of local distributors such as **Adafruit and Fry's Electronics** in the US that sell the Raspberry Pi for a margin. Please check the Raspberry Pi Foundation website and other sources for more vendors.

Requirements to get started with the Raspberry Pi

In this section, we will discuss the items required to get started with the Raspberry Pi. We will need all the same things that are required to use a computer/laptop. They are:

- ▶ Display
- ▶ Keyboard
- ▶ Mouse
- ▶ Wi-Fi Adapter / Ethernet cable

It is possible to use the Raspberry Pi via remote login using a secure shell. This might seem difficult to those who are new to the Linux environment. The setup of the Raspberry Pi for remote login is explained in *Project 13*, *Tips and Tricks*.

The Raspberry Pi eLinux wiki (`http://elinux.org/RPi_Hub`) has listed peripherals that have been tested and confirmed to have worked on the Raspberry Pi. You have the freedom to choose peripherals according to your choice.

- ▶ **Display**: The Raspberry Pi is provided with an HDMI output and an RCA output. It is possible to connect a monitor that has an HDMI input. It is also possible to connect monitors that have a DVI input with an HDMI to the DVI cable.

- ▶ **Power supply**: Since the Raspberry Pi consumes 700 mA for its operation, it is recommended that the reader uses powered USB hubs to use devices such as Wi-Fi adapters as opposed to plugging in devices such as the Wi-Fi adapters directly to the USB port of the Raspberry Pi to avoid the device resetting itself.

Operating systems on the Raspberry Pi

The Raspberry Pi foundation recommends the following operating systems on the Raspberry Pi. They are:

- ▸ Raspbian
- ▸ Arch Linux ARM
- ▸ RISC OS

You are welcome to choose any operating system of your choice. For beginners, we strongly recommend the Raspbian OS for projects. The Raspbian is equipped with tools to get started easily. The Raspberry Pi's firmware is implemented such that the operating system is loaded from an SD card.

Getting started with Raspbian

In this section, we will download an image from the Raspberry Pi Foundation's webpage to a computer, flash an SD card with the image, and set up the operating system on the Raspberry Pi. We will also try to write and execute our first example.

Downloading Raspbian

The latest Raspbian image is hosted on the Raspberry Pi Foundation's webpage (`http://www.raspberrypi.org/downloads/`). The latest image at the time of writing this book was **Raspbian wheezy**. We need to download the image and extract it to the folder of our choice.

Raspbian wheezy on the Raspberry Pi Foundation's website

Flashing image on to the SD card

We will discuss flashing the SD card with the Raspbian image on both Windows and Linux machines.

Windows

Extract the files to a location of your choice. The **Win32DiskImager** tool is required to prepare the SD card with the Raspbian image.

[A standard Raspbian image is about 1.8 GB big. It is strongly recommended that you use an SD card that is at least of 4 GB big.]

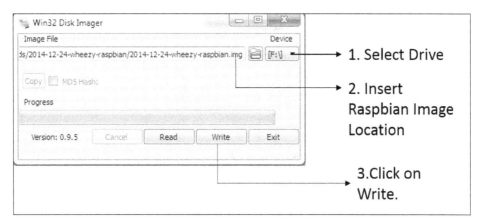

The Win32DiskImager tool

We can flash the SD card in three simple steps (as shown in the preceding screenshot):

1. Select the SD card that needs to be flashed.

2. Select the Raspbian image location.

3. Click on **Write**.

4. Click on **Yes** to confirm.

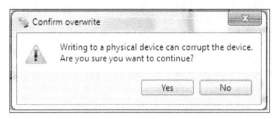

Confirm overwriting the SD card

5. It can take a while before the write cycle is completed.

Linux

There are two identical methods to flash an SD card on a Linux machine. The two approaches include:

▶ A GUI-based approach

▶ A command-line interface-based approach

A command-line interface-based approach

The SD card can be flashed in three simple steps using a command-line interface. These steps are as follows:

1. Identify the SD card mount point.

2. Unmount the SD card.

3. Flash the SD card.

Identifying the SD card mount point

As soon as we insert the SD card into a USB card reader or an SD card slot found on a laptop, we need to open a terminal on our Linux machine. We need to identify our device's mount point on the machine using the following command:

```
df -h
```

The devices enumerated on the machine will be listed as shown in the following screenshot:

```
guest-ZLhCre@sai-VirtualBox: ~
guest-ZLhCre@sai-VirtualBox:~$ df-h
df-h: command not found
guest-ZLhCre@sai-VirtualBox:~$ df -h
Filesystem      Size   Used Avail Use% Mounted on
/dev/sda1       123G   4.5G  112G   4% /
udev            1.8G   4.0K  1.8G   1% /dev
tmpfs           705M   760K  704M   1% /run
none            5.0M      0  5.0M   0% /run/lock
none            1.8G   152K  1.8G   1% /run/shm
none            100M    48K  100M   1% /run/user
none            1.8G   1.1M  1.8G   1% /tmp/guest-ZLhCre
/dev/sdb5       3.8G    41M  3.7G   2% /media/guest-ZLhCre/01CDC8FDDC8B7320
guest-ZLhCre@sai-VirtualBox:~$
```

Storage devices identified by the operating system

Unmount the SD card

In the previous example, the /dev/sdb5 path is the storage device of interest. There may be more than one storage device that might be connected to a machine. We need to make sure that we have identified the right device. Once we have identified the device, it has to be unmounted using the following command:

```
umount /dev/sdb
```

Flash the SD card

Now, we will flash our SD card using the following command:

```
dd bs=4M if=~/2012-09-18-wheezy-raspbian.img of=/dev/sdb
```

The if= argument points to the location of the image and of= refers to the SD card mount point. The write operation takes a while to complete and it is ready for use on the Raspberry Pi upon completion.

GUI-based approach

On a Debian Linux-based operating system, there is a package called `usb-imagewriter`. The **ImageWriter** package performs the same operations required to flash an SD card.

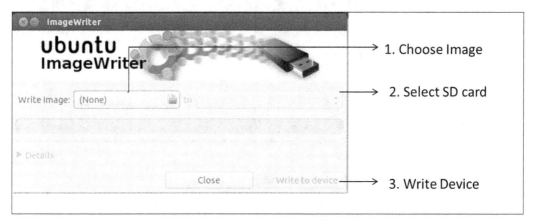

1. Choose Image

2. Select SD card

3. Write Device

A USB **ImageWriter** on Ubuntu

Setting up the Raspberry Pi

Now that the image is flashed, let's get started with setting up the Raspberry Pi for the first time. We will have to insert the SD card slot found on the other side of the Raspberry Pi.

A flashed SD card in the slot

When the keyboard and the mouse are connected, we can get started by powering up the Raspberry Pi!

Once the Raspberry Pi is powered up, the operating system boots up to **Raspi-config**. The `raspi-config` is the tool used to set up desktop options, keyboard settings, storage settings, and so on. The **Raspi-config** screen is shown in the following screenshot:

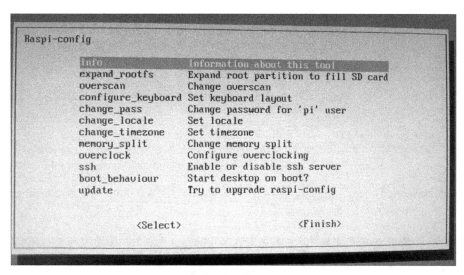

The Raspi-config screen

In this section, we will discuss each feature of the `raspi-config` tool:

- ► `info`: As the name suggests, this section gives the general information about the tool.

- ► `expand_rootfs`: While the SD card is flashed with the operating system image, the SD card is partitioned just about the size of the image. This command aids to expand the partition so that the remaining space can be used for file storage.

- ► `overscan`: This is an option used when the Raspberry Pi is connected to the television.

- ► `configure_keyboard`: This option is used to configure the `change_type` option of the keyboard.

- ► `change_pass`: The default password is *raspberry*, and if necessary, this option lets you switch to a stronger password.

- ► `change_locale`: The option lets you change the language preferences.

- ▶ `change_timezone`: We can set our current time zone using this option.
- ▶ `memory_split`: This option lets us split the memory between the ARM processor's CPU and the graphics processor.
- ▶ `overclock`: The default clock speed is 700 MHz. This option lets you set the clock speed to 1 GHz. This might vary for Raspberry Pi 2.
- ▶ `ssh`: This option enables the secure shell server. This is required to remotely log in the Raspberry Pi and control devices remotely. It is enabled by default on Raspbian.
- ▶ `boot_behaviour`: This option enables you to boot directly into the desktop.

> It is important that you enable this option on as the default option boots into a normal text-based console.

- ▶ `update`: If the Raspberry Pi is connected to the Internet using an Ethernet cable, the `raspi-config` tool downloads any package that might be available.

Once we complete the setup process by selecting **Finish**, the Raspberry Pi reboots and expands the filesystem if necessary.

Mission briefing

In this project, we will set up the **GPIO** (**General Purpose Input Output**) peripheral on the Raspberry Pi and write our first program to cause an LED to blink. At the end, we will repeat the same steps with a Raspberry Pi add-on board called PiCrust. This will allow you to get your feet wet and ensure you have all the right tools going forward, and should you need to, troubleshoot any problems you might identify.

Why is it awesome?

Think of saying "Hello World" as both a nod to programming tradition and a dry run to ensure you are well equipped!

Your Hotshot objectives

The objectives for this mission are quite simple, and yet take us all several milestones further! Here are the objectives of the Hello World mission:

- ▶ Collect all the necessary tools
- ▶ Set up the GPIO peripheral
- ▶ Introduce ourselves to the Raspberry Pi environment
- ▶ Turn a light emitting diode (LED) on and off with a 1 second delay

Mission checklist

Go over the previous sections, and make sure you have all the tools. Download the GPIO libraries, and ensure you can log in to the Raspberry Pi remotely, and you are all set!

There are two different ways to use a Raspberry Pi. They are:

> ▶ Connecting a monitor to the HDMI port or the RCA jack and a keyboard to the USB port of the Raspberry Pi.
> ▶ Remotely logging into the Raspberry Pi from the reader's workstation.

If you are a beginner, it is best to use the first method while the second method can be used if you are familiar with the Linux operating system and remote login capabilities.

Once we complete the setup process by selecting **Finish**, the Raspberry Pi reboots and expands the file system if necessary.

Hunting and gathering

As stated before, you will need to make sure you have all the tools. So, go ahead, hunt and gather away. Grab at least one of each of the following and more than one of each, if you, like us, are prone to accidents:

- ▶ A laptop to download the Raspberry Pi image and set up everything
- ▶ Raspberry Pi—Model B/B+ (preferred), a keyboard, and a mouse for the Raspberry Pi (optional)
- ▶ SD card with 4GB memory (SD card preparation was explained earlier in this project)
- ▶ USB Power Adapter (Rated 1.0 A) and Micro USB power cable
- ▶ Ethernet cable
- ▶ Wi-Fi adapter—(optional) refer to the eLinux wiki for Raspberry Pi for verified peripherals
- ▶ Breadboard
- ▶ Jumper wires
- ▶ Discrete Resistor Values
- ▶ A work bench (or a clean working surface—hopefully you have one)
- ▶ Good thoughts and a can-do attitude
- ▶ Lots of coffee, tea, or a safe beverage of your choice

Engage thrusters

You will need all of the tools listed in the previous section to get through this project. Take your time and make sure you have everything handy!

Objective complete – mini debriefing

Do you have all the tools? Ready to go? Then on to the next task!

Setting up the GPIO

We need to enable the GPIO peripherals in our Raspbian installation to get started. In order to download the required tools and set things in motion, the Raspberry Pi needs to be connected to the Internet.

The GPIO pin is a pin that is available from the Raspberry Pi's processor that enables interfacing input and output devices to the Raspberry Pi. In this section, we will talk about setting up the GPIO for interfacing an output device. There is a 26-pin interface (40 in Model B+) available on the Raspberry Pi and about 17 of those 26 pins are GPIO pins (26 of them in Model B+) while the others are miscellaneous pins such as power. The pins are driven by a 3.3 V rail and each GPIO pin is rated for about 17 mA and the total current draw not exceeding 50 mA.

Engage thrusters

We also need to know the GPIO peripherals available to conduct our experiment. The following figure shows the GPIO maps of the Raspberry Pi **Rev 1** and **Rev 2**:

GPIO map for Models A, B, and B+. (Image published with permission from Raspi.tv)

The letter **P1** shown in the following image corresponds to P1-1 of the GPIO map. P1-1 corresponds to the first pin on the left in the front row, while P1-2 corresponds to the first pin on the left in the back row.

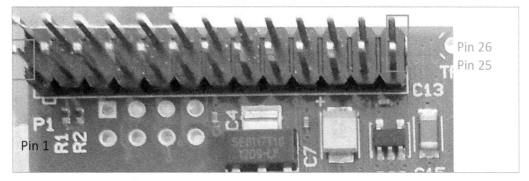

The Raspberry Pi GPIO peripheral

In this book, we will be mostly using Python programming language. Python is a very simple and easy language to learn. We may wander off to other programming languages from time to time, but we will mostly stick to Python. With this in mind, let's get started.

Installing GPIO libraries

There are a lot of libraries available to access the GPIO peripheral. The easiest to install and use is the **quick2wire python API**. The API is used to control the GPIO peripherals and I2C devices connected to the Raspberry Pi.

> There are different libraries such as the RPi.GPIO, Pi4J, and so on. We are using the **quick2wire** API in this example as a beginner might find it easy to use. You are welcome to use other libraries of your choice. The quick2wire-gpio-admin tool enables controlling the GPIO pins without root access.
>
> One disadvantage of using the quick2wire module is that it provides access only to GPIO pins 0 through 7.

The terminal can be located in the left corner of the desktop and has been highlighted in the following screenshot:

A Command-line terminal on the Raspbian desktop

4. The quick2wire library installation is based on a post on the quick2wire website (`http://quick2wire.com/articles/how-to-add-quick2wire-as-a-raspbian-software-source/`). In order to install the quick2wire-python library, the repository needs to be added to `/etc/apt/sources.list`.

> ❑ In the command line, the repository is added by using the `nano` text editor:
>
> `sudo nano /etc/apt/sources.list`

> ❑ The following lines need to be added to the file:
>
> `# Quick2Wire Software`
>
> `deb http://dist.quick2wire.com/raspbian wheezy main`
>
> `deb-src http://dist.quick2wire.com/raspbian wheezy main`

> ❑ The file can be saved by typing *CTRL+X*. The file can also be saved by pressing *Y* key while exiting the editor.

> ❑ Alternatively, the lines can be added using a graphical text editor such as, leafpad and saving it:
>
> ```
> sudo leafpad /etc/apt/sources.list
> ```

5. In order to ensure that the packages are downloaded from the quick2wire repository, we need to authenticate the packages using a key available from quick2wire:

```
wget https://raw.githubusercontent.com/quick2wire/quick2wire-
software-users/master/software@quick2wire.com.gpg.key
```

```
sudo apt-key add software@quick2wire.com.gpg.key
```

6. The cache is updated and the latest software packages can be downloaded as follows:

```
sudo apt-get update
```

```
sudo apt-get upgrade
```

7. The quick2wire tool is installed as follows:

```
sudo apt-get install quick2wire-gpio-admin
```

```
sudo apt-get install quick2wire-python3-api
```

Objective complete – mini debriefing

Now, wasn't that easy? Let's get more familiar with the GPIO input/output operations.

GPIO programming using Python

In this section, we will ensure that the library is correctly installed and add the user to the group. This will enable the user to use the GPIO pins without having root privileges. This will be followed by the section on getting started with GPIO control programming in Python.

Engage thrusters

In order to get started with programming in the Raspberry Pi, we will launch Python IDLE3 from the desktop.

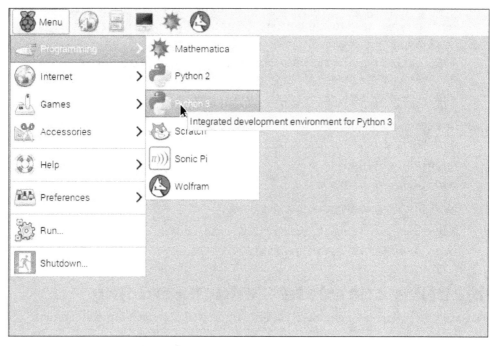

Launching IDLE3 from the desktop

1. Now, we have to get started with programming the LED blinking example in IDLE3.

2. This LED blinking sample code is as follows:

```python
from time import sleep
from quick2wire.gpio import pins, Out

with pins.pin(7, direction=Out) as out_pin:
    while True:
        out_pin.value = 1
        sleep(1)
        out_pin.value = 0
        sleep(1)
out_pin.unexport()
```

3. We will import the `sleep` class from the `time` module in the first line. This is required to introduce a 1-second delay between turning the LED on and off every other second:

```
from time import sleep
```

4. We also need the pin class from the `quick2wire` GPIO library:

```
from quick2wire.gpio import Pin
```

5. We need to set the output pin that we will be using in the example:

```
LED_output = Pin(8, Pin.Out)
```

6. We can set the pin to the logical high (3.3 V) as follows:

```
LED_output=1
```

7. We will set the pin to the logical low (0 V) as follows:

```
LED_output=0
```

8. We will execute the same thing using an infinite `while` loop:

```
while True:
    LED_output=1
    sleep(1)
    LED_output=0
    sleep(1)
```

9. This will make the LED blink with a 1-second delay. We should also note the indent on the blink sequence. The blink sequence has a different indent compared to the `while` loop. Hence, the code that is at a different indent is executed infinitely.

10. When the program is interrupted (by pressing *CTRL + C* on the keyboard), we need to unexport the pins at exit:

```
out_pin.unexport()
```

An alternative to quick2wire – RPi.GPIO

1. Another alternative is to use RPi.GPIO (https://pypi.python.org/pypi/RPi.GPIO). It comes as a standard package along with the Raspbian Wheezy OS. Let's perform a quick review of the code:

```
import RPi.GPIO as GPIO
from time import sleep

GPIO.setmode(GPIO.BCM)
GPIO.setup(8,GPIO.OUT)
```

```
GPIO.output(8,GPIO.LOW)

while True:
    GPIO.output(8,GPIO.HIGH)
    sleep(1)
    GPIO.output(8,GPIO.LOW)
    sleep(1)

GPIO.cleanup()
```

2. After importing the required modules, we get started with setting up the pin numbering mode. There are two types of pin numbering modes, namely:

   ❑ **The BCM Pin numbering mode**: The pin numbers are based upon the pin numbers of the BCM chip.

   ❑ **The Board numbering mode**: The pin numbers are based upon the pin numbers of the Raspberry Pi GPIO header.

   ❑ In this example, we will set the BCM numbering mode and set pin 8 as the output:

```
GPIO.setmode(GPIO.BCM)
GPIO.setup(8,GPIO.OUT)
```

3. We can set the pin to logical high (3.3 V) as follows:

```
GPIO.output(8,GPIO.HIGH)
```

4. We can set the pin to logical low (3.3 V) as follows:

```
GPIO.output(8,GPIO.LOW)
```

5. Now, the LED can be made to blink with a 1 second delay:

```
while True:
    GPIO.output(8,GPIO.HIGH)
    sleep(1)
    GPIO.output(8,GPIO.LOW)
    sleep(1)
```

6. When the program is interrupted by typing *CTRL + C*, we have to clean up and release any occupied GPIO resources:

```
GPIO.cleanup()
```

Objective complete – mini debriefing

In this section, we finished writing a program to make an LED blink. In the next section, we will put a circuit together that makes an LED blink.

Electrical output of our program

In the previous section, we wrote a program to make an LED blink. Let's look at the electrical connection to observe the output of our program. We will connect a resistor between the GPIO pin and the anode of the LED. We will connect the cathode to the ground pin of the Raspberry Pi.

Engage thrusters

We will connect the LED and the resistor to the GPIO pin and the ground pin, as shown in this image:

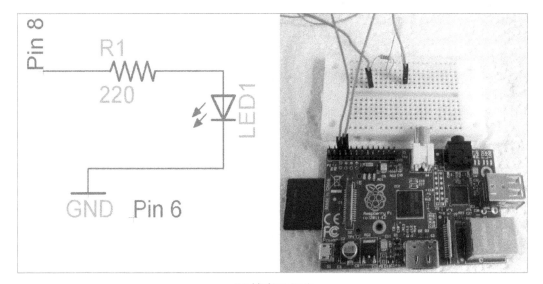

LED blinking circuit

 If we are not careful with the handling of the Raspberry Pi GPIO pins, it may either temporarily reset the Raspberry Pi or sometimes even permanently damage the GPIO pin. There are several tutorials in basic electronics available over the Web. It is important that you familiarize yourself with the basics of electronics.

Once we connect the circuit as shown in the preceding image, we will be able to execute the program and conclude our experiment.

We can execute the program by running the module, as shown in the following screenshot:

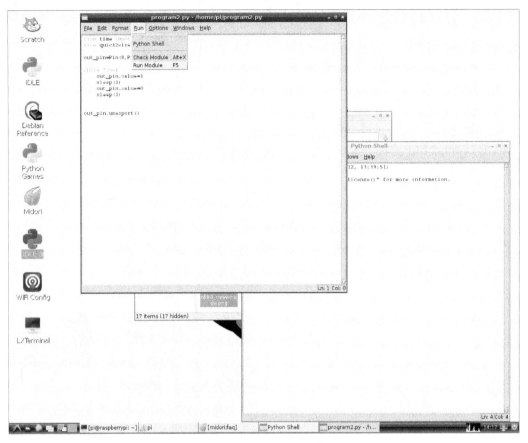

Executing the Python example

Objective complete – mini debriefing

That's it! We have wet our feet by saying Hello World by blinking an LED! On our way to bigger and better things, let's stop and examine the **Pi Crust** for a moment.

Introduction to the Pi Crust – a prototyping platform for the Raspberry Pi

Now that our Hello World example is done, we will leave you with one more thing. Throughout this book, we will review some add-on hardware to access the GPIO peripherals on the Raspberry Pi. In this project, we will discuss the Pi Crust board for the Raspberry Pi.

The Pi Crust board was designed by Joe Walnes. It is a board that is stackable on the Raspberry Pi and eliminates the need for a breadboard to prototype circuits.

A Pi Crust board

The Pi Crust is an open source add-on hardware and costs approximately $14 to build one ourselves. The design can be downloaded free of cost from http://picru.st.

So, it is up to you to decide whether you want to simply buy one, build one, or as we are prone to encourage, improve upon it and open source it for others to benefit!

The main advantage behind Pi Crust is that it is aids prototyping. It allows easy access to the I2C interface, SPI interface, UART port, and the GPIO pins. The following figure shows **BlinkM**—an I2C-driven RGB LED mounted on top of the Pi Crust.

Pi Crust stacked on top of the Raspberry Pi

Mission accomplished

Now that you have traveled this far with us, how do you feel? Do you need a break, or more coffee? Before you do either, let's review.

In this project, we got started with the LED blinking example using the Raspberry Pi. We discussed the setup of GPIO peripherals and using them in an experiment. You are welcome to continue experiments with the GPIO peripherals with projects such as LED sequencing, three bit counter, and so on.

In the forthcoming projects, we will look into I2C communication, SPI communication, and UART communication (serial port).

Hotshot challenge

Well done; you have taught your Pi to say "Hello World"! However, we are sure you can do more, much more. Have you watched the movie *Close Encounters of the Third Kind*? Well, if not, you should. However, this is not a challenge in itself. In the movie, the human beings attempt at communication with what they believe is aliens by building a pattern of lights that are set to music. Can you make a pattern of LEDs repeat that or something similar?

Project 2

A Raspberry WebIDE Example

In this project, we will learn how to develop projects using the WebIDE from Adafruit Industries. We will flash an SD card with the Raspbian OS, install the Occidentalis tool (`https://learn.adafruit.com/adafruit-raspberry-pi-educational-linux-distro/occidentalis-v0-dot-3`), set up the web-based development tool, and test the setup using an example.

 Occidentalis was initially available as a Raspbian OS image by Adafruit Industries. It comprised of the toolset that enabled to get started with project development using the Raspberry Pi. The OS image was deprecated and released after we finished writing the book. We have taken our best effort to update the book. Please refer to this book's website for more information.

Mission briefing

In this project, we will discuss installing a tool, **Occidentalis**, and a WebIDE that enables programming in the Python language on the Raspberry Pi. We will also discuss one example from the Adafruit repository and another example of driving an RGB LED.

The following table lists the bill of materials used in this project. These are just examples, and alternative products that have a similar specification may also be used.

Item	Estimated Cost
Raspberry Pi Model B	35 USD
Adafruit Cobbler (`https://www.adafruit.com/product/914`)	7 USD
Adafruit 7-segment LED Backpack (`https://www.adafruit.com/product/879`)	10 USD
Blinkm (`https://www.sparkfun.com/products/8579`)	13 USD

Why is it awesome?

The Adafruit WebIDE in combination with the Occidentalis operating system enables development in the Python language on a Raspberry Pi using just a web browser. It also enables access to sample projects developed by Adafruit via Bitbucket, a source control tool. (If you are not familiar with source control tools such as Bitbucket, Git, and so on, the examples in this project are a great way to get started!) The Adafruit WebIDE is a tool developed for hobbyists and comes with examples for techniques such as pulse-width modulation (used in lighting system control) and I2C communication, and also provides examples for controlling products from Adafruit.

The Adafruit WebIDE is now a beta release and it may not work successfully across different platforms. The Adafruit learning system has indicated that this development tool was directed towards advanced hobbyists. We have taken our best efforts to explain it as simply as possible.

Pulse-width modulation is a technique used widely in motor control, lighting systems, and so on. It is a technique where the average voltage applied to a device is varied by changing the width of the pulse. There are several tutorials on pulse-width modulation (`https://learn.sparkfun.com/tutorials/pulse-width-modulation`) available all over the Web.

I2C communication (`https://learn.sparkfun.com/tutorials/i2c`) is a form of serial communication interface used to connect multiple slave devices (usually sensors) with a master device (Raspberry Pi or a microcontroller) through a common interface.

Your Hotshot objectives

In this project, we will discuss the following features:

- ▶ Bootstrapping your Raspberry Pi by installing Occidentalis
- ▶ Setup of remote login into the Raspberry Pi
- ▶ Installation of the Raspberry Pi WebIDE
- ▶ Python development on the WebIDE
- ▶ Test and debugging examples using the WebIDE

 This project should not be considered as an attempt to promote Adafruit Industries or their products developed for their platform. This project merely demonstrates simplification of development on the Raspberry Pi using a tool from Adafruit Industries.

Mission checklist

In order to get started, the first step is to install the Occidentalis distro, which is a derivative of the Raspbian operating system.

The things required to get started are as follows:

- ▶ A 4 GB SD card flashed with the Raspbian OS
- ▶ An Occidentalis image.
- ▶ An Ethernet cable

Installation, features, and usage of the Occidentalis operating system from Adafruit

The first step is installing Occidentalis on the Raspberry Pi.

Prepare for lift off

The first step is the installation of the Adafruit-Pi-Finder tool. The tool can be downloaded from `https://github.com/adafruit/Adafruit-Pi-Finder/releases/latest`. It is available for Windows, Linux, and Mac platforms.

Engage thrusters

1. You can find detailed instructions on installing the Occidentalis tool at `https://github.com/adafruit/Adafruit-Pi-Finder`.

2. Alternatively, a step-by-step instruction is also available on this book's website. We cannot include them here since changes were made to Occidentalis installation process after we finished writing this book.

Objective complete – mini debriefing

Once the installation is complete, we have to ensure that the Raspberry Pi as well as the development machine are connected to the network via the Ethernet port or a USB Wi-Fi dongle.

Setup of a remote login into the Raspberry Pi

In this section, we will remotely log in to the Raspberry Pi using a secure shell. Since the Raspberry Pi comes with `sshd` enabled, it is possible to log in remotely using the local name, `raspberrypi.local` (During the bootstrapping process, the `avahi-daemon` tool is installed and hence, it is possible to remotely log in to the Raspberry Pi using the local name, `raspberrypi.local`). Alternatively, on a Windows machine, you can use a tool such as Advanced IP Scanner (`http://www.advanced-ip-scanner.com/`) to find the IP address of the Raspberry Pi. A snapshot of this tool is shown later in this project.

 If you are using a Windows machine, the Bonjour Print Services drivers have to be installed to remotely log in using the local name, `raspberrypi.local`. The Bonjour Print Services drivers are available from `http://support.apple.com/kb/DL999`.

Prepare for lift off

The IP address of the Raspberry Pi can be identified using tools such as Advanced IP Scanner, as shown in the following screenshot:

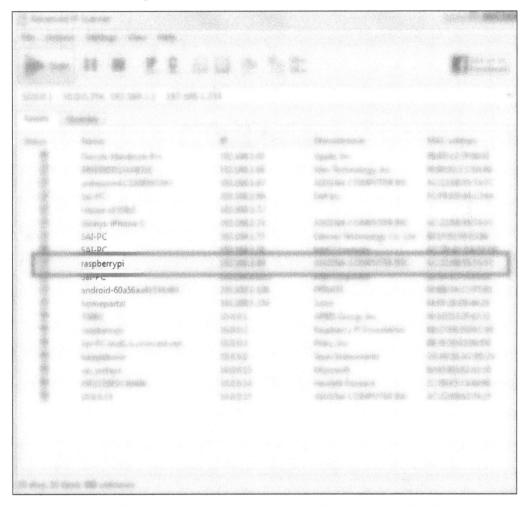

A list of devices and IP addresses connected to a network similar to the Raspberry Pi

Engage thrusters

1. Once we know the IP address, we use an SSH client such as PuTTY on Windows or a command-line terminal on a Linux or a Mac machine to remotely log in to the machine (in this case, we show this on a Windows machine).

2. On a Windows machine, we either use the IP address of the Raspberry Pi or its local name (`raspberrypi.local`) and log in to the Raspberry Pi, as shown in the following screenshot:

3. Once we enter the IP address / local name in the PuTTy window, we log in as follows:

```
login as: pi
<username>@<ip address>'s password: raspberry
```

Alternatively, we can also log in using the IP address of the Raspberry Pi instead of the local name, `raspberrypi.local`.

Objective complete – mini debriefing

If the username and password are entered correctly, we should be able to remotely log in to the Raspberry Pi to install the web server.

Installation of the Raspberry Pi WebIDE

We will get started by using a remote login client such as PuTTY to remotely log in to the Raspberry Pi and install the Adafruit WebIDE. In order to get started with examples from the Adafruit repository, we need a Bitbucket account, and Adafruit provides detailed instructions for this at `http://learn.adafruit.com/webide/getting-started`.

Engage thrusters

1. Once we have logged in, the Adafruit learning system's website recommends executing the following to install the web server:

   ```
   curl https://raw.githubusercontent.com/adafruit/Adafruit-WebIDE/
   master/scripts/install.sh | sudo sh
   ```

2. It should take about five minutes to finish the installation. If the installation was successful, we should be able to see the message marked in the following screenshot:

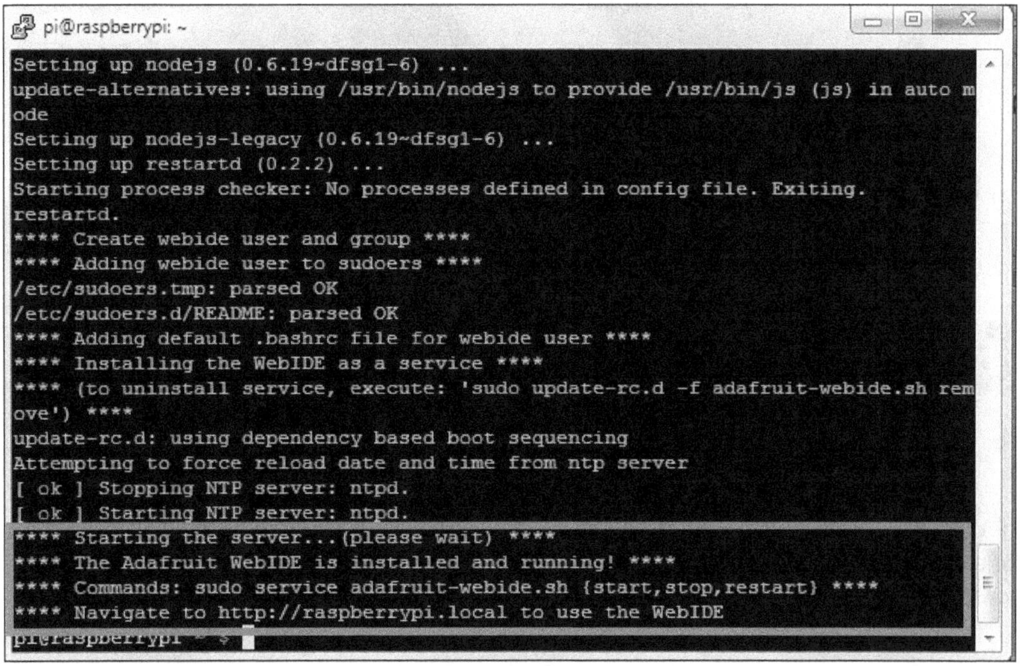

Successful completion of the Adafruit WebIDE installation

3. Assuming the installation was successful, we should be able to launch the Adafruit WebIDE using `http://raspberrypi.local`.

Adafruit WebIDE launched for the first time

4. In order to make use of the examples from Adafruit Industries, we need to create a Bitbucket account (it is possible to create one with a Google account) and integrate the WebIDE with the Bitbucket account. The instructions for this are provided on the web page, as shown in the preceding screenshot.

Objective complete – mini debriefing

If the installation was successful, after completion of the registration, we are done with this task. Let's move on and learn to code using the WebIDE!

Python development on the WebIDE

In this section, we will use a 7-segment LED backpack and the Adafruit Cobbler along with a 26-pin ribbon cable. We will test an example from the Adafruit repository (`https://github.com/adafruit/Adafruit-Raspberry-Pi-Python-Code`). In this project, the new add-on hardware that we will discuss is the Adafruit Cobbler. The Cobbler is a small board that aids prototyping circuits on a breadboard. The Adafruit Cobbler costs about 7 USD while the ribbon cable costs about 3 USD and the 7-segment backpack costs about 10 USD.

The earlier mentioned products are merely examples to demonstrate the Adafruit WebIDE. There are alternative prototyping platforms and products available for a higher or lower price.

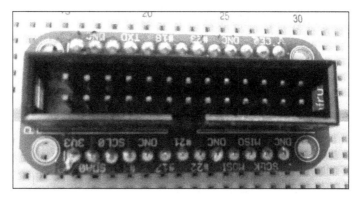

The Cobbler mounted on a breadboard

Prepare for lift off

In order to get started with the prototyping, the 26-pin ribbon cable is used to connect the GPIO interface to the Cobbler, as shown in the following image. We have to ensure that pin 1 of the GPIO header matches pin 1 of the Adafruit Cobbler. (The Cobbler comes with a shrouded header, and hence it is foolproof. However, pin 1 of the Raspberry Pi needs to be matched correctly.)

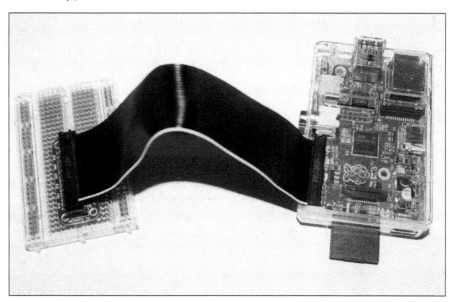

Quick introduction to the I2C interface

The I2C interface was invented by Phillips Semiconductors. It is a form of serial communication interface used to connect multiple slave devices (usually sensors) with a master device (Raspberry Pi or a microcontroller) through a common interface. Each device has a unique address that is used by the master to read or write data. There are plenty of resources available to familiarize ourselves with the I2C interface. We will move on to the next stage of configuring the interface.

Configuring the I2C interface on the Raspberry Pi

In the Occidentalis distribution, the I2C drivers are installed and enabled by default. Hence, we can get started by connecting the Adafruit 7-segment backpack to the Adafruit Cobbler, as shown in the following image. (Connections between the Cobbler and the 7-segment backpack are Clock pin, SCL (C)-SCL(B) Data Pin - SDA(C) -SDA(B), 3V3(C) to +(B) GND(C) to -(B), where C is the Cobbler and B is the backpack):

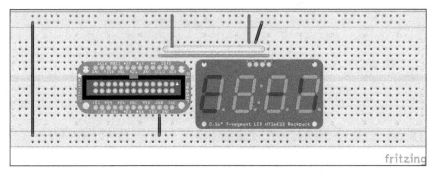

7-segment backpack connections on a breadboard

Now that we have connected the Raspberry Pi, the Adafruit Cobbler, and the 7-segment backpack, let's get started with the detection of the backpack on the Raspberry Pi's I2C interface and program an example.

Before we get started with the example, we need to determine the I2C bus to which the device is connected by using the following command:

```
sudo i2cdetect -y 0
```

The command outputs a table that contains the list of devices for that particular bus. Since there are no devices connected to bus 0, we scan for devices on bus 1. In this experiment, we are testing the Adafruit 7-segment backpack. In the figure that follows, the 7-segment backpack is connected to bus 1 and the device address is **0x70**. Refer to the following screenshot:

The i2cdetect output

We should change the bus address in the code to drive the 7-segment backpack. Line 11 in the `Adafruit_I2C.py` file needs to be changed in the code according to the bus to which the device is connected. Hence, line 11 should be:

```
def __init__(self, address, bus=smbus.SMBus(1), debug=False):
```

Engage thrusters

1. The 7-segment backpack is a device controlled via an I2C port. Any I2C device has four pins, namely clock, data, power supply, and ground. The I2C device needs to be connected to the Cobbler, as shown in the earlier screenshot.

2. There are several examples available from Adafruit in the WebIDE. Let's locate the `ex_7segment_clock.py` example (in the IDE, it is located at `Adafruit_Raspberry-Pi-Python-Code | ex_7segment_clock.py`). This is a simple example to display the current time on the 7-segment backpack:

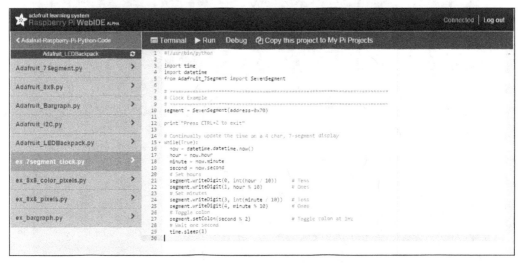

The ex_7segment_clock.py file location in the WebIDE

3. Let's do a quick review of the program. We get started by importing the `datetime` and `Adafruit_7Segment` modules:

❏ The `segment` variable is initialized as an instance of an I2C device at the address 0x70. We enter an infinite loop and get the current time using the `datetime` module:

```
now = datetime.datetime.now()
hour = now.hour
minute = now.minute
second = now.second
```

❏ Since the 7-segment LED backpack consists of four digits, we write the current time at each position as follows along with a colon:

```
# Set hours
  segment.writeDigit(0, int(hour / 10))      # Tens
  segment.writeDigit(1, hour % 10)           # Ones
  # Set minutes
  segment.writeDigit(3, int(minute / 10))    # Tens
  segment.writeDigit(4, minute % 10)         # Ones
```

```
# Toggle colon
segment.setColon(second % 2)                    # Toggle colon
at 1Hz
# Wait one second
```

❑ This exercise is repeated with a one second interval.

4. The program is executed by clicking on **Run** found in the IDE. If our connections were right, we should be able to see the current time on the 7-segment display (shown in the following figure).

Objective complete – mini debriefing

We were able to test an Adafruit product using their WebIDE in this section.

A 7-segment backpack connected to the Cobbler

Test and debugging examples using the WebIDE

In this example, we will connect the **BlinkM** to the Raspberry Pi. A BlinkM is an RGB LED that can be connected to your Raspberry Pi via the I2C interface. It is possible to execute light scripts using the port. The connections to the BlinkM are similar to that of the 7-segment backpack.

BlinkM connected to the Cobbler

It is important to pay attention while connecting devices to the GPIO header of the Raspberry Pi. If there are devices that draw a lot of current from the GPIO pins, it may reset the Pi or permanently damage it in the event of a short circuit. It is assumed that you are familiar with basic electronics and capable of handling such devices.

Prepare for lift off

Similar to the previous experiment, we need to determine the bus to which the device is connected using the `i2cdetect` command. As shown in the following screenshot, the device is connected to bus 1 and the device address is **0x09**:

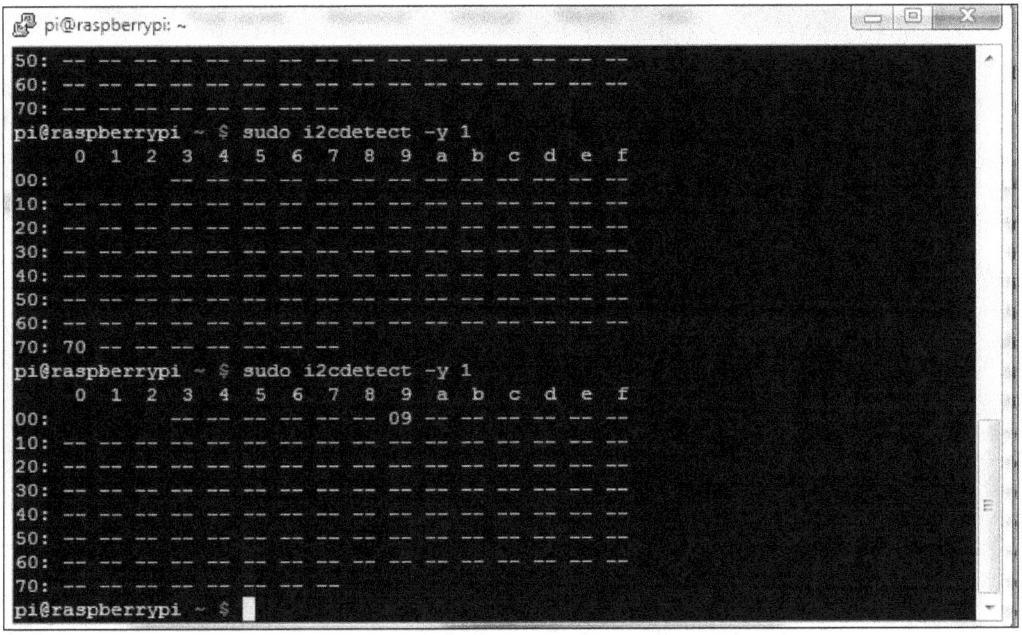

Blinkm connected to bus 1

Engage thrusters

1. The BlinkM datasheet (`thingm.com/fileadmin/thingm/downloads/BlinkM_datasheet.pdf`) provides step-by-step information to execute the light scripts.

2. A list of scripts available on the BlinkM is shown in the following screenshot:

Id	Description	Color sequence
0	eeprom script default startup	white→red→green→blue→off (can be programmed)
1	RGB	red→green→blue
2	white flash	white→off
3	red flash	red→off
4	green flash	green→off
5	blue flash	blue→off
6	cyan flash	cyan→off
7	magenta flash	magenta→off
8	yellow flash	yellow→off
9	black	off
10	hue cycle	red→yellow→green→cyan→blue→purple
11	mood light	random hue→random hue
12	virtual candle	random yellows
13	water reflections	random blues
14	old neon	random orangeish reds
15	the seasons	spring colors→summer→fall→winter
16	thunderstrom	random blues & purples→white flashes
17	stop light	red→green→yellow
18	morse code	S.O.S in white

A list of scripts available on the BlinkM

3. Let's see the code to execute a light script (for example, script number 6) on the BlinkM using the Adafruit WebIDE interface. In order to execute a script forever, the datasheet mentions that the following characters should be written at the I2C device address in the following sequence: `'p', <script no>, 0, 0`. Let's discuss how to execute this using a Python script on the Raspberry Pi interfaced with the BlinkM LED. The Python script of this example is called `Play_blinkm.py`:

   ❑ The `Play_blinkm.py` file can be executed by creating a new file in the repository that was created when you signed up for a Bitbucket account. When the file is saved, the changes are saved to your Bitbucket account. The code for this is given as follows:

```python
#!/usr/bin/python
#python-smbus
import smbus
#create i2c object
```

```
bus = smbus.SMBus(1)
#refer to datasheet for script sequence
#Play script by writing 0x70 or p on the bus
bus.write_byte(0x09,0x70)
#play script no:6
bus.write_byte(0x09,0x06)
#play the script infinitely
bus.write_byte(0x09,0x00)
bus.write_byte(0x09,0x00)
```

❑   The first line of this code is called **shebang**. It indicates that the script has to be executed using Python.

❑   We need to import `python-smbus` to execute the light script:

```
import smbus
```

❑   We need to create an object for I2C communication. We need to write the control script via bus 1. This is done by the following line of code:

```
bus = smbus.SMBus(1)
```

❑   In order to play a script (script number 6 in this case) forever, we write `'p',<script no>,0,0` on the I2C bus as follows:

```
bus.write_byte(0x09,0x70)
bus.write_byte(0x09,0x06)
bus.write_byte(0x09,0x00)
bus.write_byte(0x09,0x00)
```

4.   This would cause the BlinkM to execute script number 6 as long as the device is powered and until another instruction has been issued to the device through the I2C interface.

5.   Now, it is possible to debug our program by executing it step by step. This helps identify any problems with the program. Let's review some options to debug a program. We can launch the program for troubleshooting/debugging by clicking on **Debug**.

The Adafruit WebIDE toolbar

- This opens up two consoles, **Debug Output** and **Debug Variables** (shown in the following screenshot). The window **Debug Output** prints any output of the program. If we included any print statements in our program, the output is displayed in this window. This window can be used to view any results, ensure that a particular callback function was executed, or determine whether the program execution got past a particular line of the program.

- The **Debug Variables** window displays the state of variables as the program is being executed. Both the windows are helpful in determining whether a Python script was written as intended.

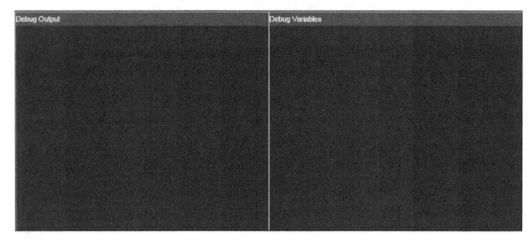

Debug terminals

- When we start debugging a Python script, the toolbar at the top presents us with two options, namely **Step Over** and **Step In**, as shown in the following screenshot:

The Adafruit debug toolbar

- In this example, it is possible to test the execution of commands by stepping through each line of the script. This is really useful when devices (for example, a pressure sensor) are not providing the intended output to identify the root cause.

Objective complete – mini debriefing

In this section, we interfaced and controlled an RGB LED using an I2C interface and discussed some options available for debugging in the Adafruit WebIDE.

The Adafruit WebIDE can considerably reduce the turnaround time for any project development activity.

Mission accomplished

In this project, we worked on two simple experiments using the I2C interface on the Raspberry Pi. The two examples discussed using the Adafruit WebIDE reflect the fact that the tool can help save time for any electronics project involving a Raspberry Pi since it comes with some of the prerequisites installed along with a web interface that just makes remote development easier.

We hope that you had fun taking the Occidentalis distribution for a test drive and find it useful in your projects.

Hotshot challenge

In this project, we used two different types of I2C devices, that is, an LED backpack and an RGB LED. It is possible to connect multiple I2C devices to the same interface. How can this be achieved? How can we identify the addresses of these I2C interface-enabled devices and control them?

Project 3
The Arduino Raspberry Pi Interface

In this project, we will look into interfacing the Raspberry Pi to the Arduino microcontroller development platform. Arduino (`www.arduino.cc`) is a popular microcontroller platform that is widely used to prototype different projects. We will discuss installation of the Arduino development environment and discuss an example of its usage.

Raspberry Pi and Arduino have become popular platforms among hobbyists, and it is being widely used by people from different backgrounds, including school and university students, artists, and engineers. This project explains how the Raspberry Pi can be used in combination with Arduino.

 The Raspberry Pi comes with a GPIO pin set that is quite capable of interfacing and control devices. We would like to discuss the Arduino Raspberry Pi interface because you may have projects that were originally built using an Arduino, especially in scenarios where a remote firmware update needs to be performed on the Arduino platform using the Raspberry Pi. This project presents the options of enhancing the capabilities of the Arduino microcontroller using a Raspberry Pi.

Mission briefing

In the first part of the project, we will discuss programming the Arduino for the first time, and in the second half, we will look into the control of a *Weasley weather clock*. We will also look into the **Raspberry Pi AlaMode** , stackable add-on arduino hardware (`http://wyolum.com/projects/alamode/`).

Why is it awesome?

Arduino is an open source microcontroller development platform based on the **Atmel** series of microcontrollers. It has brought engineers, artists, and students to the same table. The programming interface (programs are written in C/C++ usually) is so simple and this was the sole reason that made the platform so popular. Hence, it is widely used for prototyping in product development.

Over the years, there have been several hardware add-ons that aided in hardware development using the Arduino. Some of these add-ons can be stacked on top of the Arduino development platform, and they are commonly referred to as **shields**. There are shields for medical devices, interfacing sensors, GPS units, and actuators such as stepper motors, servo motors, and so on. The ecosystem of the gadgets that are built around the Arduino is so vast that the microcontroller platform was launched into the stratosphere along with a helium balloon.

Where can you buy an Arduino?

Since the Arduino is an open source microcontroller board, there are many resellers for the product. The basic version of the Arduino is the Arduino Uno and costs about $29.95. Arduino-related products are sold at websites such as Sparkfun, Adafruit, and Seeed Studio.

Your Hotshot objectives

In this project, we will do the following:

- ▶ Install the Arduino IDE
- ▶ Program the Arduino using the Raspberry Pi
- ▶ Raspberry Pi AlaMode (or any other Arduino development board)
- ▶ Introduction to Weasley Weather Clock and Bill of Materials
- ▶ Control the stepper using the Arduino
- ▶ Control the RGB LED Strip using the Arduino
- ▶ I2C Communication using the Arduino (optional)
- ▶ Serial port communication with the Raspberry Pi

Mission checklist

We need a Raspberry Pi along with an SD card flashed with the Raspbian OS, a micro USB power cable, display setup, and an Arduino to get started. In the later section of this project, we will need some additional hardware such as RGB LED Strips, motors, wires, and so on.

Installing the Arduino IDE

In this section, we will install the Arduino IDE on the Raspberry Pi.

Prepare for lift off

An Arduino microcontroller development platform (any variant that could be programmed using the Arduino IDE is fine) is absolutely essential for this section of the project.

Engage thrusters

1. The IDE could be installed by executing the following command in the command line terminal:

    ```
    sudo apt-get install arduino
    ```

2. Most Arduino products come with a USB port and are programmed via the USB port (the Arduino enumerates as a serial port device) . It takes a while to download and install the Arduino IDE. Once the installation is finished, we can test the installation by executing the following command:

    ```
    arduino
    ```

    ❑   The Arduino IDE is shown in the following screenshot:

The Arduino IDE interface

Objective complete – mini debriefing

Now that we have installed the Arduino IDE, let's move on to the next section and run an example test using the Arduino development platform.

Programming the Arduino using the Raspberry Pi

We will introduce ourselves to the Arduino IDE with an LED blinking example.

Prepare for lift off

There are several examples for the Arduino and it takes less than a minute to execute the first program. Let's get started with the traditional LED blinking example. The LED blinking example can be found at `File | Examples | 01.Basics | Blink`.

Engage thrusters

1. We get started by identifying the Arduino's serial port enumerated on the Raspberry Pi.

2. The serial port is identified from **Tools | Serial Port**. Usually there is only one serial port as shown in the following screenshot. If there is more than one serial port device connected, it is recommended that you proceed with caution.

3. We can program the Arduino by clicking on the **Upload** button.

The Arduino IDE interface

Objective complete – mini debriefing

If the Arduino is connected and the serial port was correctly identified, the program should be uploaded successfully.

```
// the loop routine runs over and over again forever:
void loop() {
  digitalWrite(led, HIGH);   // turn the LED on (HIGH is the voltag
  delay(1000);               // wait for a second
  digitalWrite(led, LOW);    // turn the LED off by making the volt
  delay(1000);               // wait for a second
}
```

Done uploading.

Binary sketch size: 1,072 bytes (of a 32,256 byte maximum)

1   Arduino Uno on /dev/ttyACM0

Sketch uploaded using the Arduino IDE

Most Arduino products come with an onboard LED to test the LED blinking example.

Raspberry Pi AlaMode

In this section, we will briefly discuss the Raspberry Pi AlaMode's features and its setup. Raspberry Pi AlaMode (as shown in the following figure) is a stackable Arduino development platform developed specifically for the Raspberry Pi. The board, which is released as open source hardware, is priced at about $45 and also includes a real-time clock and a micro SD card slot for data logging.

Raspberry Pi AlaMode mode stacked on the Raspberry Pi

Prepare for lift off

The attractive feature of the board is that it could be programmed via the Raspberry Pi's UART pins and hence eliminates the need for a USB port. The board could be either powered via the Raspberry Pi or through the Micro B USB port using a wall wart transformer. The product's webpage, `http://wyolum.com/projects/alamode/alamode-getting-started/`, offers a single step process to start using the board.

> The Raspberry Pi AlaMode mode is just one example of the stackable Arduino hardware. There are probably other similar stackable Arduino hardware available in the market. For example, `https://www.kickstarter.com/projects/raspitv/raspio-duino-affordable-arduino-programming-on-ras`.

Engage thrusters

1. Once the archive is downloaded from their web page, we extract the contents:

    ```
    tar -xvzf alamode-setup.tar.gz
    ```

2. Once the files are extracted, the setup is as follows:

    ```
    sudo ./setup
    ```

3. After the installation is complete, the Raspberry Pi a la mode's serial port is enumerated as */dev/ttyS0*.

Objective complete – mini debriefing

After the installation is complete, we should have the Raspberry Pi AlaMode mode enumerated and be ready to start programming the hardware add-on board.

The Weasley weather clock

We will build a **Weasley weather clock** in this project using an Arduino microcontroller board and the Raspberry Pi. The Weasley Weather clock is inspired by the Weasley clock seen in the Harry Potter series of movies. A Weasley clock is used to identify the current location of a family member of the Weasleys (for example, work, school, and so on) and also the safety of the family member. Mrs. Molly Weasley (the matriarch of the Weasleys) used the Weasley clock to keep tabs on her family and this clock has had its variants over the years. This project happens to be one of them!

The Weasley weather clock is one that displays the current outdoor temperature and the forecast. It also warns us about impending dangers due to conditions such as tornadoes, blizzards, and so on.

A Weasley weather clock built using the Arduino and the Raspberry Pi

Prepare for lift off

The following items (along with their approximate cost) are required to build our Weasley clock:

Item	Price
Raspberry Pi model B * 1	US$ 35
Arduino Uno/Raspberry Pi AlaMode mode (http://wyolum.com/projects/alamode/) *1	US$ 30/45
Acrylic Sheet 24 inchesx20 inches*0.093 inch thick *1	US$ 10
Wood sheet 1ftx 1/2ftx0.25 inch thick *1	US$5
5V DC Stepper motor from Adafruit *1 (http://www.adafruit.com/product/858)	US$ 5
RGB LED Strip 1 m *1 (analog ones (http://www.adafruit.com/products/1004))	US$ 15
NPN transistors *2 (BC547 or NP2222)	US$1
Power Darlington Stepper Driver (ULN2003A)	US$2
Cables for connection	US$4

Item	Price
7-Segment Backpack (http://www.adafruit.com/product/879)	US$10
A 8x8 LED Matrix backpack (optional (http://www.adafruit.com/product/871))	US$10
BlinkM (optional)	US$13
12V, 1A DC wall transformer (optional (https://www.sparkfun.com/products/8579))	US$8
Total cost	US$ 122 approx.

Engage thrusters

1. The Weasley clock could be easily assembled with parts machined with a laser cutter.

    ❏   Laser cutting is a process where parts are machined/engraved/cut using a high-power laser beam in a controlled environment.

    ❏   The laser cutter is widely used for prototyping purposes. The design files for laser cutting are available along with this book code bundle.

    ❏   In this example, the dial of the weather clock is cut from the acrylic and the design includes mounting holes for the clock as well as the stepper motor.

    ❏   The weather keywords are engraved and machined using wood sheets. The assembly of the keywords and the dial are shown in the following figure:

Partial assembly of the Weasley Clock

Objective complete – mini debriefing

The assembly shown in the image is sufficient to test this example. You can add more features to the design. For example, you can add slots on the acrylic board to embed a 7-Segment display, 8x8 LED matrix, or a BlinkM RGB LED to the design.

In this example, the Arduino is the low-level controller, which drives the RGB LED strip, stepper motor, and so on, while the weather data is obtained from the Internet using the Raspberry Pi. We will discuss the Arduino code in the first part of our task.

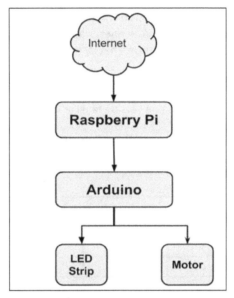

Flow of data and control in this Weasley Clock project

Controlling the stepper using the Arduino

The part number of the stepper motor used in this example is *28BJY-48* (http://www.adafruit.com/product/858). A stepper motor is a type of motor that is operated by energizing its coils in several steps. The coil energization in several steps enables the stepper to rotate in precise angular steps. This precise movement aids the use of a stepper motor in open loop systems. Since the working principle of a stepper motor is beyond the scope of the book, let's discuss its control technique.

Prepare for lift off

The stepper motor is powered by a common lead connected to the power supply and the other end is connected to a transistor. Since transistors can be used as switches, the leads of the coil can be grounded alternatively. This alternative sequence causes the stepper motor to rotate and the speed of rotation is controlled by introducing a delay in between the coil energization. The minimum delay required between each energization step to make the stepper rotate properly and avoid misssteps is 2 milliseconds. This is due to the design limitations of the stepper motor.

The following table shows the coil energization sequence for the stepper motor in a clockwise direction (borrowed from the datasheet). The energization sequence shown here would make the stepper rotate in a half step per actuation, that is, the stepper would rotate 2.8125 degrees for every actuation sequence.

 It is assumed that you are familiar with stepper motors and their control theory.

SWITCHING SEQUENCE

Lead Wire Color	---> CW Direction (1-2 Phase)							
	1	2	3	4	5	6	7	8
4 ORG	-	-						-
3 YEL		-	-	-				
2 PIK				-	-	-		
1 BLU						-	-	-

A stepper motor energization sequence from 28BJY-48's datasheet

Engage thrusters

1. Each column in the preceding diagram indicates the lead that needs to be energized to rotate a single step.

2. For example, in the case of clockwise rotation, Lead 4 is energized and all other leads are turned off. The datasheet explains that the stepper motor rotates approximately 5.625 degrees per step.

3. Hence, 64 actuation steps are required (*64*5.626 = 360 degrees*) to make one complete rotation. The stepper motor is interfaced to a gearbox of 1:64 ratio, and each rotation takes about 4096 steps.

4. Let's review the code required for the energization sequence (code borrowed from the Arduino forums `http://forum.arduino.cc/index.php?topic=85335.0`):

```
// Step 1
digitalWrite(motorPin4, HIGH);
digitalWrite(motorPin3, LOW);
digitalWrite(motorPin2, LOW);
digitalWrite(motorPin1, LOW);
delay(motorSpeed);
//Step 2
digitalWrite(motorPin4, HIGH);
digitalWrite(motorPin3, HIGH);
digitalWrite(motorPin2, LOW);
digitalWrite(motorPin1, LOW);
delay (motorSpeed);
//Step 3
digitalWrite(motorPin4, LOW);
digitalWrite(motorPin3, HIGH);
digitalWrite(motorPin2, LOW);
digitalWrite(motorPin1, LOW);
delay(motorSpeed);
//Step 4
digitalWrite(motorPin4, LOW);
digitalWrite(motorPin3, HIGH);
digitalWrite(motorPin2, HIGH);
digitalWrite(motorPin1, LOW);
delay(motorSpeed);
//Step 5
digitalWrite(motorPin4, LOW);
digitalWrite(motorPin3, LOW);
digitalWrite(motorPin2, HIGH);
digitalWrite(motorPin1, LOW);
delay(motorSpeed);
//Step 6
digitalWrite(motorPin4, LOW);
digitalWrite(motorPin3, LOW);
digitalWrite(motorPin2, HIGH);
digitalWrite(motorPin1, HIGH);
delay (motorSpeed);
//Step 7
digitalWrite(motorPin4, LOW);
digitalWrite(motorPin3, LOW);
digitalWrite(motorPin2, LOW);
digitalWrite(motorPin1, HIGH);   delay(motorSpeed);
```

```
//Step 8
digitalWrite(motorPin4, HIGH);
digitalWrite(motorPin3, LOW);
digitalWrite(motorPin2, LOW);
digitalWrite(motorPin1, HIGH);
delay(motorSpeed);
}
```

5. Let's discuss the first step in the stepper motor energization sequence:

```
// Step 1
digitalWrite(motorPin4, HIGH);
digitalWrite(motorPin3, LOW);
digitalWrite(motorPin2, LOW);
digitalWrite(motorPin1, LOW);
delay(motorSpeed);
```

6. In the preceding lines of code, the `motorPin4` pin is set to `High`, while the other pins are set to `Low`. As shown in the following figure, the pins `motorPin1` through `motorPin4` are connected to a power Darlington circuit. You can find a reference to the Power Darlington circuit at `https://coefs.uncc.edu/dlsharer/files/2012/04/F5.pdf`.

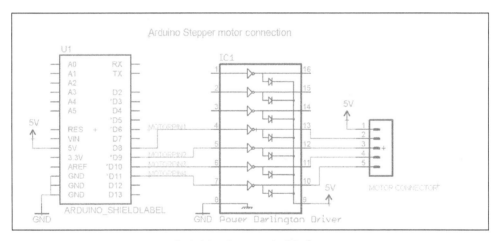

An Arduino stepper motor interface

7. When `motorpin4` (the D11 pin of the Arduino is connected to the base pin of the power Darlington pair) is set to `high`, the transistor (which acts a switch) connects the orange lead to the ground and energizes the coil and thereby the stepper moves by a single step.

8. Similarly, the stepper motor's coils are energized in the sequence shown in the table. For example, in step 2, the coils 4 and 3 are energized by setting `motorPin4` and `motorPin3` to High and other pins to Low.

Counterclockwise rotation of the stepper motor

1. The counterclockwise rotation is achieved by reversing the order of energization. In the first step, Lead 1 is energized, which is followed by Leads 1 and 2. The table for counterclockwise rotation is shown as follows:

Lead Wire Color	CCW Direction							
	1	2	3	4	5	6	7	8
1 BLU	-	-						
2 PIK		-	-	-				
3 YEL				-	-	-		
4 ORG						-	-	-

2. Hence, the code for the first step will be as follows:

```
digitalWrite(motorPin1, HIGH);
digitalWrite(motorPin2, LOW);
digitalWrite(motorPin3, LOW);
digitalWrite(motorPin4, LOW);
delay(motorSpeed);
```

Objective complete – mini debriefing

 If you are not familiar with stepper motors and their control techniques, there are abundant resources and one such resource is http://www.societyofrobots.com/ member_tutorials/node/314.

We discussed the stepper motor control technique using the Arduino microcontroller. Once we have discussed the prerequisites, we will take this code sample and build things around it.

Controlling the RGB LED Strip using the Arduino

We depict the mood of the weather forecast by using RGB LED lighting. We indicate cold weather indications with blue color lighting, fair weather conditions with green lighting, and warm/dangerous weather conditions using red lighting. In this section, we will look into controlling an RGB LED using the Arduino.

The RGB LED strip sold by Adafruit industries (`http://www.adafruit.com/products/1004`) consumes about 60 mA per segment. It is best recommended to drive the RGB LED strip using a transistor switching circuit. We need to use three transistors for the three colors and it is possible to control each color individually and it is also possible to obtain a combination of colours.

 It is possible to produce a secondary color using the RGB combinations. This can be achieved by turning on the RGB segments at the same time and varying the brightness of the primary colors. There are vast resources available for such tips and tricks on the Internet and an explanation of this is beyond the scope of this book.

Prepare for lift off

The Adafruit learning website provides examples for controlling the RGB LED using a pulse width modulation technique. The schematic for the Analog RGB strip is shown in the following diagram:

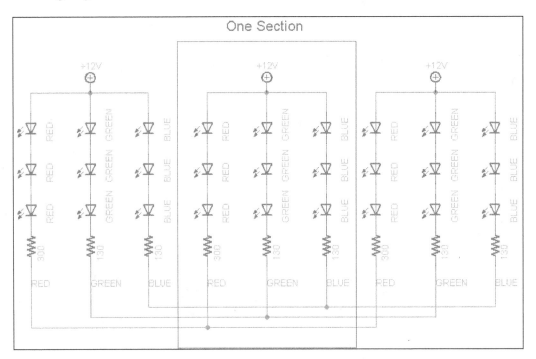

RGB LED strip schematic (borrowed from Adafruit)

Since the RGB strip requires 12 V, we must use a transistor switching circuit to control the LEDs. The transistor switching circuit for controlling the Red, Green, and Blue channels of the LED strip is shown in the following diagram:

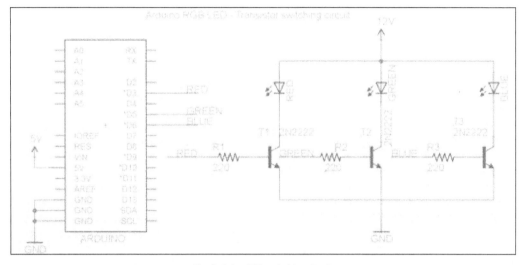

The Arduino RGB switching circuit

The RGB channels are connected to the NPN transistors that act as switches. The base of the transistor is connected to the **PWM (Pulse Width Modulation)** output of the Arduino. This enables you to adjust the brightness of the RGB channels, and consequently, produce different colors.

Engage thrusters

1. Adafruit has provided an example for adjusting the brightness of the LEDs and producing different colors from the combination of primary colors. Let's consider the following piece of code:

```
// fade from blue to violet
  for (r = 0; r < 256; r++) {
    analogWrite(REDPIN, r);
    delay(FADESPEED);
  }
  // fade from violet to red
  for (b = 255; b > 0; b--) {
    analogWrite(BLUEPIN, b);
    delay(FADESPEED);
  }
```

2. In this code, the red, green and blue segments of the RGB LED strip are connected to the **D3**, **D5**, and **D6** of the Arduino, respectively.

   ❑ The value written to the pins using the `analogWrite` function sets the brightness value of each color.

   ❑ The `analogWrite` function varies the duty cycle of the PWM channel and accepts values between 0 and 255.

   ❑ The value 0 indicates a 0 percent duty cycle and 255 indicates a 100 percent duty cycle. The duty cycle determines the current that flows through the LED, and in turn, controls the brightness and color.

Objective complete – mini debriefing

We discussed adjusting the brightness of the RGB LED strip using the Pulse Width Modulation Technique and an Arduino microcontroller-based development platform.

I2C Communication using the Arduino (optional)

In this project, there is a 7-Segment display, 8x8 LED matrix, proximity sensor (to determine the home position), and a BlinkM RGB LED that communicates via the I2C interface. We will discuss the application of each component in this project.

Prepare for lift off

The main requirement for this section is the necessary I2C device required to interface with the weather clock.

Engage thrusters

Let us review about the 7-Segment display.

The 7-Segment display

1. The Adafruit 7-Segment display backpack (reference: the tutorial available at `https://learn.adafruit.com/adafruit-led-backpack/0-dot-56-seven-segment-backpack` provides instructions on setting up the backpack and testing the backpack with a code sample), which is used to display the current atmospheric temperature obtained via the Raspberry Pi.

2. Adafruit provides libraries to write to the 7-Segment display. In order to write to the 7-Segment display, we declare a 7-Segment object:

```
Adafruit_7segment matrix_7segment = Adafruit_7segment();
```

❑ We initialize the I2C port address of the device in the Arduino `setup()` function:

```
matrix_7segment.begin(0x70);
```

❑ Now, we can call the object and write data on the display (code borrowed from Adafruit LED backpack libraries):

```
matrix_7segment.clear();
matrix_7segment.print(temp, DEC);
matrix_7segment.writeDisplay();
```

8x8 LED matrix

1. The Adafruit 8x8 matrix is used to display the mood of the current weather condition using a smiley. (The setup tutorial can be found at `https://learn.adafruit.com/adafruit-led-backpack/0-8-8x8-matrix`).

2. If the current weather condition is fair, a smile is displayed and a frown is displayed for impending danger.

3. The write process is similar to the 7-Segment display. The 7-Segment display and the 8x8 display matrix use the MAX7219 chip. Hence, it is necessary to use a different address for the LED matrix. The Adafruit tutorial (`https://learn.adafruit.com/adafruit-led-backpack/connecting-multiple-backpacks`) clearly explains how to change I2C port addresses on the LED backpack. You are welcome to switch the address if both the 7-Segment display and the LED matrix are being used in the project.

4. It is also possible to write strings to the 8x8 matrix and scroll like a marquee. Similar to the 7-Segment display, we will initialize the object to communicate with the LED matrix:

```
Adafruit_8x8matrix matrix = Adafruit_8x8matrix();
```

❑ We initialize the I2C port address of the device in the Arduino `setup()` function:

```
matrix_7segment.begin(0x73);
```

❑ Adafruit tutorials also explain the creation of bitmaps for the smileys to be displayed:

```
static uint8_t __attribute__ ((progmem)) smile_bmp[]={0x3C,
0x42, 0x95, 0xA1, 0xA1, 0x95, 0x42, 0x3C};
static uint8_t __attribute__ ((progmem)) frown_bmp[]={0x3C,
0x42, 0xA5, 0x91, 0x91, 0xA5, 0x42, 0x3C};
```

```
static uint8_t __attribute__ ((progmem)) neutral_
bmp[]={0x3C, 0x42, 0x95, 0x91, 0x91, 0x95, 0x42, 0x3C}
```

❏ The bitmap is used to determine the LEDs that would have to be turned on to create the smiley. For example, `0x3C` (binary value: 00111100) turns on the LEDs except for the first and last two on either ends:

```
matrix.clear();
matrix.setRotation(3);
matrix.drawBitmap(0, 0, smile_bmp, 8, 8, LED_ON);
matrix.writeDisplay();
```

❏ The `setRotation` function is used to rotate the display image by 90 degrees. The `drawBitmap` function is used to draw the bitmap on the display. In the `drawBitmap` function, the first two arguments specify the *x* and *y* of the starting position followed by the bitmap, width, height of the bitmap, and its color.

BlinkM

1. We discussed the BlinkM RGB LED in *Project 2, A Raspberry WebIDE Example*. The BlinkM is used to indicate impending danger by flashing a red color in the event of impending danger. We use the BlinkM libraries to play a flashing red script in such scenarios:

```
BlinkM_playScript(script_no,0,0 );
```

2. The `BlinkM_playScript` function takes the script number of the RGB LED. The second argument is the number of repeats for the script. When the third argument is zero, the script is played in an infinite loop.

Proximity sensor

1. The proximity sensor is used to determine the home position of the arrow that is used to point to the weather position. The proximity sensor used in this project is the OSEPP Proximity Sensor Module from Parallax. The proximity sensor detects the presence of objects and communicates this via the I2C communication port.

2. Similar to the other I2C devices, we set the sensor address as follows:

```
const uint8_t sensorAddr = 0x20;
```

❏ We turn on the sensor in the Arduino `setup()` method:

```
WriteByte(sensorAddr, 0x3, 0xFE);
```

❏ The sensor's reading is read by:

```
ReadByte(sensorAddr, 0x0, &val)
```

Objective complete – mini debriefing

We discussed the interfacing of different I2C devices that could be used in this project. In the next section, we will work on controlling these devices using an individual control signal.

Serial port communication with the Raspberry Pi

As mentioned earlier, the weather data is obtained by the Raspberry Pi and communicates the data with control characters via the serial port. We will discuss the control signals used in this project.

Engage thrusters

Let's get started by reviewing the Python script used to operate the weather display.

Python program for the Weasley clock

1. In this section, we will discuss the Python code for the weather clock. The important requirement for this project is the **Python weather API**. We need to download and install it to get started. If subversion is not installed on the Raspberry Pi, it can be installed using the following command:

    ```
    sudo apt-get install subversion
    ```

2. Once the installation is complete, the Python weather API repository can be cloned as follows:

    ```
    svn checkout http://python-weather-api.googlecode.com/svn/trunk/
    python-weather-api-read-only
    ```

3. The Python weather API has a Python3 requirement and is installed as follows:

    ```
    cd python-weather-api-read-only
    python3 setup.py build
    python3 setup.py install
    ```

4. Let's review the Python script used to operate the weather display. We will import the serial port, `pywapi`, and time (for delay) modules for the project:

```
#!/usr/bin/env python
import serial
import glob
import pprint
import pywapi
from time import sleep
```

   ❑   We will determine and establish connection to the serial port. The `scan()` function identifies all the serial ports available on the Raspberry Pi:

```
# Establish serial port communication
def scan():
    return glob.glob('/dev/ttyS*') + glob.glob('/dev/
ttyUSB*')+ glob.glob('/dev/ttyACM*')
sport_data = scan()

for name in scan():
    serialport = serial.Serial(name,9600)
    sleep(5)
    serialport.write(bytes("A",'ascii'))
    sleep(1)
    response = serialport.read()
    if(response==b'A'):
        sport = name
        serialport.close()
        break
seport = serial.Serial(sport,9600,timeout=45)
```

5. Once the serial ports have been identified, we test them by sending a byte A and await a response. When a response with the byte A is received, we identify and save the serial port. After identification, we will establish a connection with the Arduino.

6. In this project, we are using the NOAA website to obtain the weather data. We have to identify the city's weather code to obtain the current location's weather station code. This could be simply obtained by entering the zip code on their website. For example, the weather station code for Chicago is *KORD*.

Weather station for Chicago, IL

❑ The weather data is obtained as follows:

```
result = pywapi.get_weather_from_noaa('KORD')
```

❑ The temperature data is retrieved as follows:

```
temperature = int(float(result['temp_f']))
```

❑ The retrieved data is written to the serial port:

```
temperature_string= "S"+str(temperature)
#print(temperature_string)
seport.write(bytes(temperature_string,'ascii'))
```

❑ Based on the temperature data, the RGB strip, BlinkM control data, and 8x8 matrix data are written to the Arduino:

```
if(temperature>40):
    seport.write(bytes("G",'ascii'))
    sleep(5)
    seport.write(bytes("P4",'ascii'))
    sleep(5)
    seport.write(bytes("M1",'ascii'))
    sleep(5)
```

❑ We will set the weather clock to point at a weather forecast based on the data obtained:

```
if(result['weather']=='Light Snow') or
(result['weather']=='Snow') or (result['weather']=='Flurri
es'):
    seport.write(bytes("H",'ascii'))
    sleep(5)
    seport.write(bytes("T-2",'ascii'))
    sleep(5)
```

7. Let's review the code for the control from the Raspberry Pi and the corresponding acknowledgment signals.

Arduino acknowledgement to control signal

Let us review on the control signal and control flow of the weather clock.

Control flow for the weather clock

The following flowchart shows what happens in the Arduino when a control character is received from the Raspberry Pi.

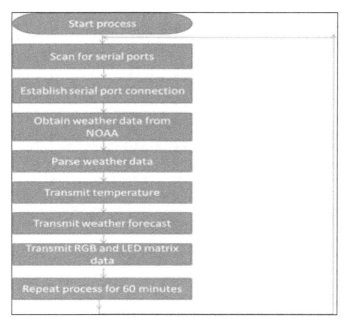

The weather clock program flow

1. The Raspberry Pi tries to identify the Arduino by sending a character A. The Arduino responds with an acknowledgement character A:

```
if(serial_read=='A'){
        Serial.print("A");
        }
```

2. This is a foolproof mechanism to identify and establish a communication with the weather clock controller from the Raspberry Pi.

Temperature data

1. The Raspberry Pi temperature data is sent to the Arduino with the letter / character S. The received data is converted to a signed integer and passed as an argument to the 7-Segment display libraries:

```
if(serial_read=='S') {
        while(Serial.available()){
        sb = Serial.read();
        sevenseg_string[serInIndx] = sb;
        serInIndx++;
        temp=0;
        }
        temp=atoi(sevenseg_string);
        memset(sevenseg_string,0,9);
        }
```

2. When the character S is received, we read all the characters into the buffer `sevenseg_string`. The string is converted to an integer using the `atoi` function and stored in the `temp` variable. The buffer is cleared at the end of the cycle. This method takes sub-zero temperatures into consideration.

Control of the RGB LED strip

1. The individual colors of the RGB LED are controlled individually using the ASCII characters R, G, and, B respectively. Each color indicates a unique weather condition, namely, blue indicates cold weather, green indicates fair weather conditions, and red color indicates impeding danger in weather conditions:

```
if(serial_read=='R' || serial_read=='G' ||
        serial_read=='B') {
        color_bit=serial_read;
        }
if(color_bit=='R'){
    lightsequence_red();
 }
 else if(color_bit=='G'){
    lightsequence_green();
```

```
    }
    else if(color_bit=='B'){
      lightsequence_blue();
    }
```

2. When the character is received, the corresponding light sequence is turned on.

Control of stepper via serial port

1. Earlier, we discussed the control of the stepper motor using a power Darlington driver and the control routine for one full rotation. In this section, we will discuss how to control the direction and the number of steps based on the input from the serial port. In this example, the clockwise direction is indicated by +, and counterclockwise direction is indicated by -.

    ❑   For example, in order to move 45 steps in a clockwise direction, the command would be *+45* preceded by the letter *P*. Hence, it would be *P+45*. Similarly, the counterclockwise direction command would be *P-45*:

```
if( serial_read == 'P' ) {
        while(Serial.available())
        {
          sb = Serial.read();
          serInString[serInIndx] = sb;
          serInIndx++;
        }
}
```

2. We await the serial character P and store the rest of the string in a buffer. Once the data is stored in the buffer, we will determine whether the first character is + or -.

    ❑   The ASCII number for the + sign is 43 and 45 for the - sign. We compare the first character in the buffer and execute the command accordingly. Serial communications usually transmit ASCII numbers and hence the numbers are converted into their decimal equivalents:

```
if(serInString[0]==43){
int var_serial=0;
    for(serOutIndx=1;serOutIndx<serInIndx;serOutIndx++)
      {
        var_serial = var_serial*10+(serInString[serOutIn
dx]-48);
      }
    motorSpeed=20;
    for(int i=0;i<var_serial;i++){
      clockwise();

    }
```

- ❑ We convert the received serial data into their decimal equivalent at this step:

```
var_serial = var_serial*10+(serInString[serOutIndx]-48);
```

- ❑ Once converted, we move the stepper for the desired number of steps in either direction using the `clockwise()` and `counterclockwise()` functions.

3. We want the stepper motor to reach the home position every time before pointing to a particular weather condition. This system is an open loop and so it is necessary to move the arrow to the home position before pointing to the current weather condition.

 The stepper motor moves in a counterclockwise direction to point at all weather conditions and a clockwise direction to move towards the home position.

4. Hence, when the letter H is transmitted via the serial port, the arrow is moved towards the home position:

```
if(serial_read=='H'){
        reset_stepper();
        lightsequence();
    }
```

- ❑ The `reset_stepper()` function takes care of setting the arrow to the home position:

```
void reset_stepper(void){
  uint8_t val;
 // Get the value from the sensor
   if (ReadByte(sensorAddr, 0x0, &val) == 0)
   {
      // The second LSB indicates if something was not
detected, i.e.,
      // LO = object detected, HI = nothing detected
      while(val & 0x2)
      {
         motorSpeed=20;
         Serial.println("Nothing detected");
         if(ReadByte(sensorAddr, 0x0, &val) == 0){
           clockwise();//We keep going clockwise until the
arrow is detected
         }
      }

   }
}
```

```
        else
        {
            Serial.println("Failed to read from sensor");
        }
}
```

❑ In the `reset_stepper()` function, we will execute the stepper motor's clockwise routine until the object is detected. The sensor reference manual mentions that an object is detected if the second LSB is set to low. Hence, the stepper rotates in the clockwise direction until a low signal is detected.

Programming the weather forecast position

1. In the previous section, we discussed the stepper motor control via the serial port. Since we are using a stepper motor, it is possible to point at each weather forecast condition based on a predetermined number of steps from the step. So, we will determine the number of steps required to point at each weather forecast condition and program these positions into the flash memory of the Arduino.

   ❑ We should use the PROGMEM keyword to store the position data in the flash memory of the Arduino since they are a constant:

   ```
   const int mydata[6][2] PROGMEM = {
           1, 10,
           2, 18,
           3, 28,
           4, 43,
           5, 54,
           6, 66};
   ```

   ❑ The numbers 1 through 6 in the array correspond to the weather forecast indicators starting in the counterclockwise direction. The second position indicates the number of positions from the home position to point to that particular weather condition.

   ❑ The command for indicating weather data is preceded by the letter T. In order to point to the weather forecast, Rain, the command would be T-6. When a character T is received, we store the data received in a buffer. It is confirmed that the second character received after the letter T is a number between 1 and 6. We will retrieve the corresponding position data from the flash memory using the pgm_read_word_near() function. Once the data is retrieved, the stepper motor control routine is executed for the desired number of steps.

❑ Now we will retrieve the data from the flash memory as follows:

```
if ( serial_read == 'T' ) {
        while (Serial.available())
        {
          sb = Serial.read();
          serInString[serInIndx] = sb;
          serInIndx++;
        }
      }
int var_serial=serInString[1]-48;
    serInIndx=0;
    if(var_serial>0 && var_serial <=6)
    {
      steps=pgm_read_word_near(&mydata[(var_serial-1)][1]);
      Serial.println(steps);
    }
    if(serInString[0]==45){

    motorSpeed=20;
    for(int i=0;i<steps;i++){
      counterclockwise();
    }
```

8x8 matrix control

▸ We will control the LED matrix using the letter M. A smile is displayed if M1 is received and a frown if M2 is received:

```
if(serial_read=='M'){
        sb=Serial.read();
        if(sb-'0'==1) {
          set_display(smile_bmp);
        }
        else if(sb-'0'==2) {
          set_display(frown_bmp);
        }
      }
```

BlinkM control

▸ The BlinkM script is played whenever the letter P is received. The letter P is followed by the script number.

```
if ( serial_read == 'P' ) {
        while (Serial.available())
        {
```

```
        sb = Serial.read();
        serInString[serInIndx] = sb;
        serInIndx++;
      }
    BlinkM_playScript( BlinkM_addr,serInString[0]-48,0,0 );
  }
```

Objective complete – mini debriefing

In this section, we discussed the overall control of the weather clock and its interface to the Internet. We also discussed the interfacing of the sensors and displaying the weather data.

Mission accomplished

In this project, we discussed interfacing an Arduino with the Raspberry Pi. This was followed by an example of constructing a weather clock. We demonstrated the Arduino as a low-level controller that interfaces actuators, sensors, and display devices while the Raspberry Pi is interfaced with the Internet. I hope you enjoyed the project!

Hotshot challenge

In this example, the city location was hard-coded into the Python script. It is possible to display the weather data based on the zipcode / city location. What could the input device be? How can this be achieved?

Project 4

Christmas Light Sequencer

As the name suggests, we will design automation and control of Christmas lights in our homes. We will decorate our homes with lights for any festive occasion and work on a project that enables us to build fantastic projects. We will build a local server to control the devices. We will use the **web.py** framework to design the web server. We'd like to dedicate this chapter to the memory of Aaron Swartz who was the founder of the web.py framework.

Mission briefing

In this chapter, we will install a local web server-based control of GPIO pins on the Raspberry Pi. We will use this web server framework to control it via a web page.

The Raspberry Pi on top of the tree is just an ornament for decoration

Why is it awesome?

We celebrate festive occasions by decorating our homes. The decorations reflect our heart and it can be enhanced by using Raspberry Pi.

 This project involves interfacing AC-powered devices to Raspberry Pi. You should exercise extreme caution while interfacing the devices, and it is strongly recommended that you stick to the recommended devices.

Your objectives

In this chapter, we will work on the following aspects:

- Interface of the Christmas tree lights and other decorative equipment to the Raspberry Pi
- Set up the digitally-addressable RGB matrix
- Interface of an audio device
- Setting up the web server
- Interfacing devices to the web server

Mission checklist

This chapter is based on a broad concept. You are free to choose decorative items of your own interest. We chose to show the following items for demonstration:

Item	Estimated Cost
Christmas tree * 1	30 USD
Outdoor decoration (optional)	30 USD
Santa Claus figurine * 1	20 USD
Digitally addressable strip * 1	30 USD approximately
Power Switch Tail 2 from Adafruit Industries (http://www.adafruit.com/product/268)	25 USD approximately
Arduino Uno (any variant)	20 – 30 USD approximately

Interface the devices to the Raspberry Pi

 It is important to exercise caution while connecting electrical appliances to the Raspberry Pi. If you don't know what you are doing, please skip this section. Adult supervision is required while connecting appliances.

In this task, we will look into interfacing decorative appliances (operated with an AC power supply) such as the Christmas tree. It is important to interface AC appliances to the Raspberry Pi in accordance with safety practices. It is possible to connect AC appliances to the Raspberry Pi using solid state relays. However, if the prototype boards aren't connected properly, it is a potential hazard. Hence, we use the **Power Switch Tail II** sold by Adafruit Industries.

 The Power Switch Tail II has been rated for 110V.

According to the specifications provided on the Adafruit website, Power Switch Tail's relay can switch up to 15A resistive loads. It can be controlled by providing a 3-12V DC signal. We will look into controlling the lights on a Christmas tree in this task.

Power Switch Tail II – image source: Adafruit.com

Prepare for lift off

We have to connect the Power Switch Tail II to the Raspberry Pi to test it. The follow Fritzing schematic shows the connection of the switch to the Raspberry Pi using Pi Cobbler. Pin 25 is connected to **in+**, while the **in-** pin is connected to the **Ground** pin of the Raspberry Pi.

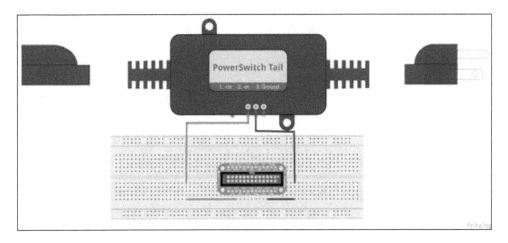

The Raspberry Pi connection to the Power Switch Tail II using Pi Cobbler

The Pi Cobbler breakout board is connected to the Raspberry Pi as shown in the following image:

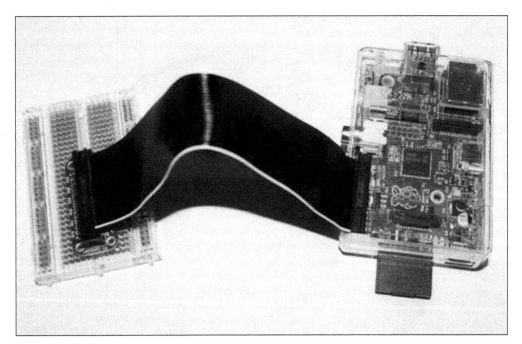

Engage thrusters

1. In order to test the device, there are two options to control the device the GPIO Pins of the Raspberry Pi. This can be controlled either using the quick2wire GPIO library or using the Raspi GPIO library.

> The main difference between the *quick2wire gpio library* and the *Raspi GPIO library* is that the former does not require that the Python script to be run with root user privileges (to those who are not familiar with root privileges, the Python script needs to be run using sudo). In the case of the Raspi GPIO library, it is possible to set the ownership of the pins to avoid executing the script as root. This is left as some homework for you.

2. Once the installation is complete, let's turn on/off the lights on the tree with a three second interval. The code for it is given as follows:

```python
# Import the rpi.gpio module.
import RPi.GPIO as GPIO
#Import delay module.
from time import sleep
#Set to BCM GPIO
GPIO.setmode(GPIO.BCM)
# BCM pin 25 is the output.
GPIO.setup(25, GPIO.OUT)
# Initialise Pin25 to low (false) so that the Christmas tree
lights are switched off.
GPIO.output(25, False)
while 1:
GPIO.output(25,False)
sleep(3)
GPIO.output(25,True)
sleep(3)
```

   ❑ In the preceding example, we will get started by importing the **raspi.gpio** module and the `time` module to introduce a delay between turning on/off the lights:

```python
import RPi.GPIO as GPIO
#Import delay module.
from time import sleep
```

❑ We need to set the mode in which the GPIO pins are being used. There are two modes, namely the board's GPIO mode and the BCM GPIO mode (more information available on `http://sourceforge.net/p/ raspberry-gpio-python/wiki/`). The former refers to the pin numbers on the Raspberry Pi board while the latter refers to the pin number found on the Broadcom chipset. In this example, we will adopt the BCM chipset's pin description.

❑ We will set the pin 25 to be an output pin and set it to `false` so that the Christmas tree lights are switched off at the start of the program:

```
GPIO.setup(25, GPIO.OUT)
GPIO.output(25, False)
```

❑ In the preceding routine, we are switching off the lights and turning them back on with a three-second interval:

```
while 1:
GPIO.output(25,True)
sleep(3)
GPIO.output(25,False)
sleep(3)
```

3. When the pin 25 is set to high, the device is turned on, and it is turned off when the pin is set to low with a three-second interval.

Connecting multiple appliances to the Raspberry Pi

Let's consider a scenario where we have to control multiple appliances using the Raspberry Pi.

It is possible to connect a maximum of 15 devices to the GPIO interface of the Raspberry Pi. (There are 17 GPIO pins on the Raspberry Pi Model B, but two of those pins, namely GPIO14 and 15, are set to be UART in the default state. This can be changed after startup. It is also possible to connect a GPIO expander to connect more devices to Raspberry Pi.)

In the case of appliances that need to be connected to the 110V AC mains, it is recommended that you use multiple power switch tails to adhere to safety practices.

In the case of decorative lights that operate using a battery (for example, a two-feet Christmas tree) or appliances that operate at low voltage levels of 12V DC, a simple transistor circuit and a relay can be used to connect the devices. A sample circuit is shown in the figure that follows:

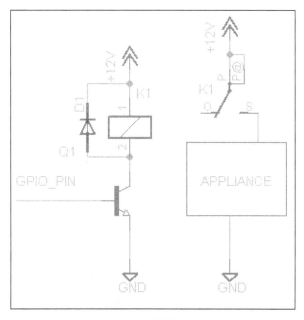

A transistor switching circuit

In the preceding circuit, since the GPIO pins operate at 3.3V levels, we will connect the GPIO pin to the base of the NPN transistor. The collector pin of the transistor is connected to one end of the relay.

The transistor acts as a switch and when the GPIO pin is set to high, the collector is connected to the emitter (which in turn is connected to the ground) and hence, energizes the relay.

Relays usually have three terminals, namely, the common terminal, Normally Open Terminal, and Normally Closed Terminal. When the relay is not energized, the common terminal is connected to the Normally Closed Terminal. Upon energization, the Normally Open Terminal is connected to the common terminal, thus turning on the appliance.

The freewheeling diode across the relay is used to protect the circuit from any reverse current from the switching of the relays.

The transistor switching circuit aids in operating an appliance that operates at 12V DC using the Raspberry Pi's GPIO pins (the GPIO pins of the Raspberry Pi operate at 3.3V levels). The relay and the transistor switching circuit enables controlling high current devices using the Raspberry Pi.

It is possible to use an array of relays (as shown in the following image) and control an array of decorative lighting arrangements. It would be cool to control lighting arrangements according to the music that is being played on the Raspberry Pi (a project idea for the holidays!).

The relay board (again, shown in the following image) operates at 5V DC and comes with the circuitry described earlier in this section. We can make use of the board by powering up the board using a 5V power supply and connecting the GPIO pins to the pins highlighted in red. As explained earlier, the relay can be energized by setting the GPIO pin to high.

A relay board

Objective complete – mini debriefing

In this section, we discussed controlling decorative lights and other holiday appliances by running a Python script on the Raspberry Pi. Let's move on to the next section to set up the digitally addressable RGB LED strip!

Setting up the digitally addressable RGB matrix

In this section, we will talk about setting up options available for LED lighting. We will discuss two types of LED strips, namely analog RGB LED strips and digitally-addressable RGB LED strips.

As we discussed the first one in detail in the previous chapter, we will skip it and move on to the second kind. A sample of the digitally addressable RGB LED strip is shown in the image that follows:

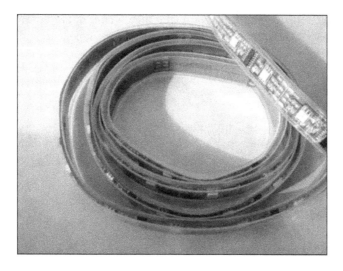

Prepare for lift off

As the name explains, digitally-addressable RGB LED strips are those where the colour of each RGB LED can be individually controlled (in the case of the analog strip, the colours cannot be individually controlled).

Where can I buy them?

There are different models of the digitally addressable RGB LED strips based on different chips such as LPD6803, LPD8806, and WS2811. The strips are sold in a reel of a maximum length of 5 meters. Some sources to buy the LED strips include Adafruit (`http://www.adafruit.com/product/306`) and Banggood (`http://www.banggood.com/5M-5050-RGB-Dream-Color-6803-IC-LED-Strip-Light-Waterproof-IP67-12V-DC-p-931386.html`) and they cost about 50 USD for a reel. Some vendors (including Adafruit) sell them in strips of one meter as well.

Engage thrusters

Let's review how to control and use these digitally-addressable RGB LED strips.

How does it work?

Most digitally addressable RGB strips come with terminals to powering the LEDs, a clock pin, and a data pin. The LEDs are serially connected to each other and are controlled through the **SPI (Serial Peripheral Interface)**.

The RGB LEDs on the strip are controlled by a chip that latches data from the microcontroller/ Raspberry Pi onto the LEDs with reference to the clock cycles received on the clock pin.

In the case of the LPD8806 strip, each chip can control about 2 LEDs. It can control each channel of the RGB LED using a seven-bit PWM channel. More information on the function of the RGB LED strip is available at `https://learn.adafruit.com/digital-led-strip`.

It is possible to break the LED strip into individual segments. Each segment contains about 2 LEDs, and Adafruit industries has provided an excellent tutorial to separate the individual segments of the LED strip (`https://learn.adafruit.com/digital-led-strip/advanced-separating-strips`).

Lighting up the RGB LED strip

There are two ways of connecting the RGB LED strip. They can either be connected to an Arduino and controlled by the Raspberry Pi or controlled by the Raspberry Pi directly.

An Arduino-based control

 It is assumed that you are familiar with programming microcontrollers, especially those on the Arduino platform.

In *Project 3*, *The Arduino Raspberry Pi Interface*, we discussed connecting an analog RGB strip using an Arduino. We used control commands to change the color of the strip through the serial port of Arduino. Similarly, we can connect the RGB strip to the Arduino.

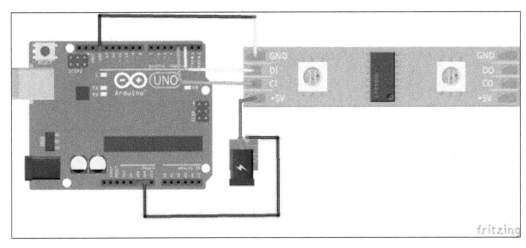

An Arduino connection to the digitally addressable interface

In the preceding figure, the LED strip is powered by an external power supply. (The tiny green adapter represents the external power supply. The recommended power supply for the RGB LED strip is 5V/2A per meter of LEDs (while writing this chapter, we got an old computer power supply to power up the LEDs). The Clock pins (the **CI** pin) and the Data pins (**DI**) of the first segment of the RGB strip are connected to the pins **D2** and **D3** respectively. (We are doing this since we will test the example from Adafruit industries. The example is available at `https://github.com/adafruit/LPD8806/tree/master/examples`.)

Since the RGB strip consists of multiple segments that are serially connected, the Clock Out (**CO**) and Data Out (**DO**) pins of the first segment are connected to the Clock In (**CI**) and Data In (**DI**) pins of the second segment and so on.

Let's review the example, `strandtest.pde`, to test the RGB LED strip. The example makes use of Software SPI (Bit Banging of the clock and data pins for lighting effects). It is also possible to use the SPI interface of the Arduino platform. (Refer to this book's website for an example.)

In the example, we need to set the number of LEDs used for the test. For example, we need to set the number of LEDs on the strip to 64 for a two-meter strip. Here is how to do this:

1. The following line needs to be changed:

   ```
   int nLEDs = 64;
   ```

2. Once the code is uploaded, the RGB matrix should light up, as shown in this image:

8 x 8 RGB matrix lit up

3. Let's quickly review the Arduino sketch from Adafruit. We will get started by setting up an LPD8806 object as follows:

```
//nLEDS refer to number of LEDs in the strip. This cannot exceed
160 LEDs/5m due to current draw.
LPD8806 strip = LPD8806(nLEDs, dataPin, clockPin);
```

4. In the `setup()` section of the Arduino sketch, we will initialize the RGB strip as follows:

```
// Start up the LED strip
  strip.begin();

  // Update the strip, to start they are all 'off'
  strip.show();
```

5. As soon as we enter the main loop, scripts such as `colorChase` and `rainbow` are executed.

6. We can make use of this Arduino sketch to implement serial port commands to control the lighting scripts using the Raspberry Pi.

This task merely provides some ideas of connecting and lighting up the RGB LED strip. You should familiarize yourself with the working principles of the RGB LED strip.

There are several examples available for controlling the LED strip using the Arduino platform. A few are available on the website of this book.

The Raspberry Pi has an SPI port, and hence, it is possible to control the RGB strip directly from the Raspberry Pi. Refer to this book's website for some examples.

Objective complete – mini debriefing

In this section, we reviewed options for decorative lighting and controlling them using the Raspberry Pi and Arduino.

Interface of an audio device

In this task, we will work on installing MP3 and WAV file audio player tools on the Raspbian operating system.

Prepare for lift off

The Raspberry Pi is equipped with a 3.5mm audio jack and the speakers can be connected to that output. In order to get started, we install the ALSA utilities package and a command-line mp3 player:

```
sudo apt-get install alsa-utils
sudo apt-get install mpg321
```

Engage thrusters

In order to use the alsa-utils or mpg321 players, we have to activate the BCM2835's sound drivers and this can be done using the modprobe command:

```
sudo modprobe snd_bcm2835
```

After activating the drivers, it is possible to play the WAV files using the aplay command (aplay is a command-line player available as part of the alsa-utils package) :

```
aplay testfile.wav
```

An MP3 file can be played using the mpg321 command (a command-line MP3 player) :

```
mpg321 testfile.mp3
```

In the preceding examples, the commands were executed in the directory where the WAV file or the MP3 file was located. In the Linux environment, it is possible to stop playing a file by pressing *CTRL + C*.

Objective complete – mini debriefing

We were able to install sound utilities in this section. Later, we will use the installed utilities to play audio from a web page.

It is possible to play the sound files on the Raspberry Pi using the module available in Python. Some examples include: Snack sound tool kit, Pygame, and so on.

Installing the web server

In this section, we will install a local web server on Raspberry Pi. There are different web server frameworks that can be installed on the Raspberry Pi. They include Apache v2.0, Boost, the REST framework, and so on.

Prepare for lift off

As mentioned earlier, we will build a web server based on the web.py framework. This section is entirely referenced from web.py tutorials (`http://webpy.github.io/`). In order to install web.py, a Python module installer such as `pip` or `easy_install` is required. We will install it using the following command:

```
sudo apt-get install python-setuptools
```

Engage thrusters

The web.py framework can be installed using the `easy_install` tool:

```
sudo easy_install web.py
```

Once the installation is complete, it is time to test it with a *Hello World!* example.

We will open a new file using a text editor available with Python IDLE and get started with a *Hello World!* example for the web.py framework using the following steps:

1. The first step is to import the web.py framework:

    ```
    import web
    ```

2. The next step is defining the class that will handle the landing page. In this case, it is `index`:

    ```
    urls = ('/','index')
    ```

3. We need to define what needs to be done when one tries to access the URL. We will like to return the `Hello world!` text:

    ```
    class index:
      def GET(self):
        return "Hello world!"
    ```

4. The next step is to ensure that a web page is set up using the web.py framework when the Python script is launched:

    ```
    if __name__ == '__main__':
      app = web.application(urls, globals())
      app.run()
    ```

5. When everything is put together, the following code is what we'll see:

```
import web

urls = ('/','index')

class index:
    def GET(self):
  return "Hello world!"

if __name__ == '__main__':
  app = web.application(urls,globals())
  app.run()
```

6. We should be able to start the web page by executing the Python script:

```
python helloworld.py
```

We should be able to launch the website from the IP address of the Raspberry Pi. For example, if the IP address is 10.0.0.10, the web page can be accessed at http://10.0.0.10:8080 and it displays the text **Hello world**. Yay!

A Hello world! example using the web.py framework

Objective complete – mission debriefing

We built a simple web page to display the **Hello world** text. In the next task, we will be interfacing the Christmas tree and other decorative appliances to our web page so that we can control it from anywhere on the local network.

It is possible to change the default port number for the web page access by launching the Python script as follows:

python helloworld.py 1234

Now, the web page can be accessed at http://<IP_Address_of_the_Pi>:1234.

Interfacing the web server

In this section, we will learn to interface one decorative appliance and a speaker. We will create a form and buttons on an HTML page to control the devices.

Prepare for lift off

In this task, we will review the code (available along with this chapter) required to interface decorative appliances and lighting arranging to a web page and controlled over a local network. Let's get started with opening the file using a text editing tool (Python IDLE's text editor or any other text editor).

Engage thrusters

1. We will import the following modules to get started with the program:

    ```
    import web
    from web import form
    import RPi.GPIO as GPIO
    import os
    ```

2. The GPIO module is initialized, the board numbering is set, and ensure that all appliances are turned off by setting the GPIO pins to low or `false` and declare any global variables:

    ```
    #Set board
    GPIO.setmode(GPIO.BCM)
    #Initialize the pins that have to be controlled
    GPIO.setup(25,GPIO.OUT)
    GPIO.output(25,False)
    ```

3. This is followed by defining the template location:

    ```
    urls = ('/', 'index')
    render = web.template.render('templates')
    ```

4. The buttons used in the web page are also defined:

    ```
    appliances_form = form.Form(
      form.Button("appbtn", value="tree", class_="btntree"),
      form.Button("appbtn", value="Santa", class_="btnSanta"),
      form.Button("appbtn", value="audio", class_="btnaudio")
    )
    ```

    ❑   In this example, three buttons are used, a value is assigned to each button along with their class.

❑ In this example, we are using three buttons and the name is appbtn. A value is assigned to each button that determines the desired action when a button is clicked. For example, when a Christmas tree button is clicked, the lights need to be turned on. This action can be executed based on the value that is returned during the button press.

5. The home page is defined in the index class. The GET method is used to render the web page and POST for button click actions.

```
class index:
  def GET(self):
    form = appliances_form()
    return render.index(form, "Raspberry Pi Christmas lights
controller")
def POST(self):
    userData = web.input()
    if userData.appbtn == "tree":
     global state
     state = not state
    elif userData.appbtn == "Santa":
#do something here for another appliance
        elif userData.appbtn == "audio":
        os.system("mpg321 /home/pi/test.mp3")
        GPIO.output(25,state)
        raise web.seeother('/')
```

❑ In the POST method, we need to monitor the button clicks and perform an action accordingly. For example, when the button with the tree value is returned, we can change the Boolean value, state. This in turn switches the state of the GPIO pin 25. Earlier, we connected the power tail switch to pin 25.

6. The index page file that contains the form and buttons is as follows:

```
$def with (form,title)

<html>
  <head>
    <title>$title</title>
    <link rel="stylesheet" type="text/css" href="/static/styles.
css">
  </head>
  <body>
    <P><center><H1>Christmas Lights Controller</H1></center>
    <br />
    <br />
    <form class="form" method="post">
    $:form.render()
    </form>
```

```
        </body>
</html>
```

7. The styles of the buttons used on the web page are described as follows in 'styles.css':

```
form .btntree {
  margin-left : 200px;
  margin-right : auto;
  background:transparent url("images/topic_button.png") no-repeat
top left;
  width : 186px;
  height: 240px;
  padding : 0px;
    position : absolute;
}
form .btnSanta{
  margin-left :600px;
  margin-right : auto;
  background:transparent url("images/Santa-png.png") no-repeat top
left;
  width : 240px;
  height: 240px;
  padding : 40px;
  position : absolute;
}
body {background-image:url('bg-snowflakes-3.gif');}
```

8. The web page looks like what is shown in the following figure:

Yay! We have a Christmas lights controller interface.

Objective complete – mini debriefing

We have written a simple web page that interfaces a Christmas tree and RGB tree and plays MP3 files. This is a great project for a holiday weekend.

It is possible to view this web page from anywhere on the Internet and turn these appliances on/off (Fans of the TV show *Big Bang Theory* might like this idea. A step-by-step instruction on setting it up is available at `http://www.everydaylinuxuser.com/2013/06/connecting-to-raspberry-pi-from-outside.html`).

Mission accomplished

In this project, we have accomplished the following:

- ▸ Interfacing the RGB matrix
- ▸ Interfacing AC appliances to Raspberry Pi
- ▸ Design of a web page
- ▸ Interfacing devices to the web page

We used examples to demonstrate the capabilities of enhancing the festive decoration using the Raspberry Pi. It is definitely possible to enhance this project using our creativity.

References

You can find web.py tutorials at `http://webpy.github.io/docs/0.3/tutorial`.

The Python Pit – Drive your Raspberry Pi with a mobile phone, MagPi February 2013 edition, page 34, (`http://www.themagpi.com/issue/issue-9/article/the-python-pit-drive-your-raspberry-pi-with-a-mobile-phone/`)

Project 5

Internet of Things Example – An E-mail Alert Water Fountain

In this project, we will work on building a water fountain enabled by Raspberry Pi. We will also decorate the fountain with lighting that can be controlled with the help of a web interface.This fountain will enable us to receive email alerts as well. It is a great example to enable the Internet of Things using the Raspberry Pi.

Mission briefing

We will learn to build a fountain and control it using a Raspberry Pi. We will build a web page based on the Flask framework and try to control the lighting arrangement on the fountain. We will demonstrate how a decorative piece, such as a tabletop fountain, can be used to receive e-mail or tweet alerts.

Following is an image that shows a fountain controlled by the Raspberry Pi:

Why is it awesome?

Tabletop fountains are soothing in effect and play a great role in relieving stress. It is fun to have a Raspberry Pi play a great role in controlling our behavior. It also enables us to remind ourselves to check our e-mails / Twitter feeds on a regular basis.

Your objectives

In this project, we will build the tabletop fountain in the following steps:

- ▸ Assembling the fountain
- ▸ Installation of the **Flask framework** and interfacing the fountain
- ▸ Controlling RGB LEDs from the web page
- ▸ Setting up e-mail alerts for the fountain

Mission checklist

A tabletop fountain can be built in several ways, and it is possible to include a lot of decorative pieces to enhance the appeal. The items listed in the following table include a basic list of items to demonstrate a fountain controlled by a Pi:

Item	Cost (approximate)
A DIY fountain kit, including container, pebbles, and so on (from home improvement companies such as Home Depot or a DIY product supplier such as American Science and Surplus).	30 USD
A submersible pump (source: same as the preceding kit).	10 USD

Item	Cost (approximate)
A digitally addressable RGB LED strip (Adafruit or Banggood. Link to sources of LED provided in the previous project).	16.00/meter USD
A wooden dowel rod (source: any hobby store).	2.00 USD
An acrylic sheet (source: any home improvement store).	12.00 USD
Mounting accessories (scotch tape and so on).	10.00 USD

In this task, we will get started with assembling the water fountain for our project. The fountain assembly is a simple three-step process. There are several resources available online to build a desktop fountain using raw materials available at home (a somewhat simple tutorial on building a tabletop fountain using a submersible from a pet store: http://www.instructables.com/id/Table-Fountain/). We will look into an example using an off-the-shelf DIY fountain kit in this step.

Prepare for lift off

If the reader is not able to gain access to a DIY fountain kit, the following items are required:

▸ A basin (preferably opaque so that it diffuses light)

▸ A fountain/submersible pump from a pet shop

▸ Pebbles and gravel

▸ Decorative accessories available from aquariums

These items could be purchased from a hobby shop or an aquarium supplies store.

Engage thrusters

1. The DIY tabletop fountain kit comes with a basin that has a provision to run the fountain pump's cable out of the basin through a sealed outlet.

A basin with a sealed electrical outlet

2.   Next, we will place the fountain pump inside the basin.

Fountain pump to be placed inside the basin

3.   We will now cover the pump with a cover and place a decorative pot.

Fountain pump covered with a decorative pot

4.   We can fill the sides of the pump with gravel, pebbles, small pieces of rock, and other decorative accessories. We then turn on the pump and test the water flow to make sure that we don't spill water and make a mess.

A fountain with decorative accessories

5. We'll wrap the fountain with a digitally addressable RGB LED strip and we are done with assembling the fountain when we power the fountain along with the RGB LEDs.

A water fountain strapped with a digitally addressable RGB LED

Objective complete – mini debriefing

In the first step, we finished assembling the fountain and the RGB LED strip. We will move on to install a web framework to implement lighting control for the framework, which we can change based on our needs.

Installation of the Flask framework

In this task, we will install the Flask framework on the Raspberry Pi and complete a test web page on the Raspberry Pi. We will use the Flask framework to control the RGB LED strip.

Prepare for lift off

In the previous projects, we installed python module installers such as `pip` or `easy_install`. If either of these tools isn't installed, they can be installed by executing the following command:

```
sudo apt-get install python-pip
```

Alternatively, you can use the following command:

```
sudo apt-get install python-setuptools.
```

Next, we will work on installing the Flask framework and the first example.

Engage thrusters

1. The Flask framework is installed using the following command:

    ```
    sudo easy_install flask
    ```

2. Once the installation is complete, we will use an example available from the Flask framework documentation (http://flask.pocoo.org/docs/0.10/quickstart/#quickstart) and create a Python script (using Python IDLE's editor):

    ```python
    from flask import Flask
    app = Flask(__name__)

    @app.route("/")
    def hello():
        return "Hello World!"

    if __name__ == "__main__":
        app.run()
    ```

3. When we execute the saved file and execute the Python script, the web server is launched locally on the Raspberry Pi:

    ```
    python helloworld.py
     * Running on http://127.0.0.1:5000/
    ```

4. The web server is only visible to the Raspberry Pi and a web page (web address: http://127.0.0.1:5000) is launched on the Raspberry Pi's browser, which will show the text **Hello World!**.

An Hello World example on the Flask framework-based web server

5. In order to make the web server visible to all devices on the local network, we need to change the following line in the Python script:

    ```
    app.run('0.0.0.0')
    ```

Objective complete – mini debriefing

In this task, we are done installing the Flask framework for controlling the framework. We will move on to the next task to set up things.

Controlling RGB LEDs from a web page

In this task, we will learn how to control the RGB LEDs from a web page. We will use the digitally controlled RGB LED strip from Adafruit Industries. We will interface a color picker and set the color of the RGB strip. The color picker wheel was borrowed from *circadian lighting project*, *Chris Fane*, distributed under MIT license. (`https://github.com/rasathus/circadianLighting`). We will modify this code sample to suit our needs. We'll also use the **LPD8806 library** written by Adam Haile, distributed under GPL v3 license. (`https://github.com/adammhaile/RPi-LPD8806.git`).

Prepare for lift off

Since we are using the digitally addressable RGB LED strip, we need to enable the SPI drivers on the Raspberry Pi.

 Enabling of SPI drivers is not necessary if the you have installed Occidentalis in *Project 2, A Raspberry WebIDE Example*.

The following file needs to be modified: `/etc/modprobe.d/raspi-blacklist.conf`.

The `blacklist spi-bcm2708` line needs to be commented out (add a # at the start of the line). Then we get the drivers working by executing the following command:

```
sudo modprobe spi_bcm2708
```

The SPI devices can be found listed in the `/dev` directory:

```
pi@raspberrypi: ~
cachefiles       mmcblk0p1          root             tty23   tty48
char             mmcblk0p2          servoblaster     tty24   tty49
console          net                shm              tty25   tty5
cpu_dma_latency  network_latency    snd              tty26   tty50
disk             network_throughput sndstat          tty27   tty51
fb0              null               spidev0.0        tty28   tty52
fd               ppp                spidev0.1        tty29   tty53
full             ptmx               stderr           tty3    tty54
fuse             pts                stdin            tty30   tty55
hidraw0          ram0               stdout           tty31   tty56
hidraw1          ram1               tty              tty32   tty57
input            ram10              tty0             tty33   tty58
kmsg             ram11              tty1             tty34   tty59
log              ram12              tty10            tty35   tty6
```

SPI devices listed in the directory

Engage thrusters

1. The Raspberry Pi needs to be connected to the SPI interface of the Raspberry Pi. The RGB LED strip has to be powered by a 5V DC adapter. The clock pin **CI** needs to be connected to the clock pin of the Raspberry Pi (pin 14, SCK pin of the Raspberry Pi).

    ❑ The clock pin **CI** needs to be connected to the clock pin of the Raspberry Pi (pin 14 of the GPIO header, **SCK** pin of the Raspberry Pi).

    ❑ The data pin **DI** (Data In) needs to be connected to the **MOSI** pin (pin 12 of the GPIO header) of the Raspberry Pi.

    ❑ The **GND** (ground pin) of the RGB LED strip needs to be connected to the **GND** (ground pin) of the GPIO header of the Raspberry Pi.

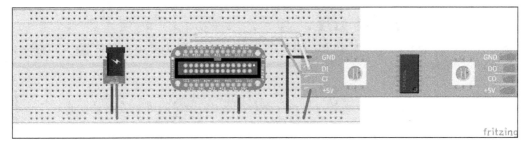

Connecting the RGB LED Strip to the Raspberry Pi using a Pi Cobbler

2. In order to control the lighting arrangement, let's make use of the Circadian lighting project's Python script and Adam Haile's LPD8806 library. We will get started by importing the Flask framework and the LPD8806 library. We will initialize the LPD8806 library by setting the number of digitally addressable RGB LEDs used in this project:

```
num = 64
led = LEDStrip(num)
```

    ❑ The circadian lighting project (http://rasathus.blogspot.com/2013/02/nasa-style-circadian-lighting-wrap-up.html) uses a color picker (based on Raphael.js) and a color is set on mouse click. The clicks on the color picker wheel are converted into RGB values as follows:

```
rgb_array = [0,0,0]
HEX = '0123456789abcdef'
HEX2 = dict((a+b, HEX.index(a)*16 + HEX.index(b)) for a in
HEX for b in HEX)

def rgb(triplet):
  triplet = triplet.lower()
  rgb_array[0] = HEX2[triplet[0:2]]
  rgb_array[1] = HEX2[triplet[2:4]]
  rgb_array[2] = HEX2[triplet[4:6]]
```

```
    return   (HEX2[triplet[0:2]],HEX2[triplet[2:4]],HEX2[tripl
et[4:6]])
def triplet(rgb):
    return format((rgb[0]<<16)|(rgb[1]<<8)|rgb[2], '06x')
```

❑ Whenever a click is detected, the posted hex values from the webserver are detected as follows:

```
@app.route('/set/<hex_val>', methods=['GET', 'POST'])
def send_command(hex_val):
rgb_val = rgb(hex_val)
```

3. The RGB values are passed to LPD8806 via the Raspberry Pi's SPI interface:

```
led.fill(Color(rgb_val[0],rgb_val[1],rgb_val[2],0.98))
led.update()
```

4. Now, when we execute the script available along in the web server sample folder, we should be able to launch a webserver that will display a colour picker as shown in the following diagram:

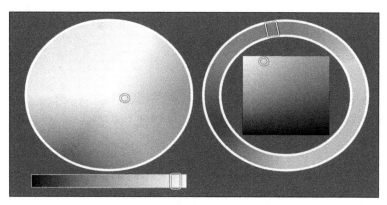

A flask framework-based RGB interface

Objective complete – mini debriefing

In this task, we finished setting up the webserver that controls the fountain. In the next task, we will review setting up e-mail alerts through colour changes on the fountain.

It is possible to control the lights of the fountain based on a song being played on the Raspberry Pi. How can this be achieved? Visit this book's website for some clues.

Setup of the e-mail alerts in the fountain

In this task, we will review setting up e-mail alerts from Gmail accounts. We can blink an LED (as shown in this step) or flash the RGB LED strip (this has to be executed by the reader) when an e-mail of a specific category is received (for example, work e-mail).

Prepare for lift off

We will get started by installing the `python-feedparser` tool. Google provides a read-only inbox feed and we will make use of the `feedparser` module to determine whether we received any new e-mails.

```
sudo apt-get install python-feedparser
```

Engage thrusters

1. In order to log in and parse through the e-mail feed, we get started by importing the `feedparser` module:

    ```
    import sys
    import feedparser
    ```

2. We will define the variables, including the Gmail username and password (changed to generic names below) along with the function that retrieves all unread e-mails. Refer to the following example:

 In this example, we are just retrieving the count of any new unread e-mails. It is possible to parse and identify e-mails with specific labels. We will leave that to the reader. For more information, refer to `https://developers.google.com/gmail/gmail_inbox_feed`.

```
newEmail=""
username="username@gmail.com"
password="password"
proto="https://"
server="mail.google.com"
path="/gmail/feed/atom"
def mail():
   email = int(feedparser.parse(proto+username+":"+password+"@"+ser
ver+path)["feed"]["fullcount"])
   return email
```

- ❑ The preceding function has been borrowed from the **WonderHowTo** website (`http://null-byte.wonderhowto.com/how-to/make-gmail-notifier-python-0132845/`).

- ❑ Let's save this function in a separate file and try to call it from another file. For example, the function has been saved in a file called `parser.py`.

3. Now, we will import the parser module by opening another file as a module and implement the e-mail notifier. In this file, we will blink an LED when there is a new e-mail. We will start by importing the `parser` module and `RPi.GPIO`:

```
import parser
import time
import RPi.GPIO as gpio
```

- ❑ We will get started by setting the output pins for the e-mail notifier example:

```
gpio.setwarnings(False)
gpio.setmode(gpio.BCM)
gpio.setup(17,gpio.OUT)
```

- ❑ Now, we'll check for new e-mails and blink an LED if there is an unread e-mail:

```
while True:
  mail = parser.mail() #check for email
  count = 0
  if mail>0:              #print for new emails
    print(mail)
    print("new emails \n")
    while count<10:
      count += 1
      gpio.output(17,gpio.HIGH) #blink LED if there are new
emails
      time.sleep(1)
      gpio.output(17,gpio.LOW)
      time.sleep(1)
    gpio.output(17,gpio.LOW) #set LED to low
  else:
    time.sleep(10) #repeat cycle for 10 seconds
```

❏ The LED needs to be connected as shown in the following figure:

A Raspberry Pi e-mail notifier – Schematic created with Fritzing, Raspberry Pi Library. Courtesy: Adafruit

In this task, we just made an LED blink when a new e-mail is received. You should try to import the LPD8806 module and flash the RGB LED strip.

Objective complete – mini debriefing

In this task, we completed the setup of the e-mail alerts as well as a user interaction element of blinking an LED. This brings us to the end of the assembly and setup of the fountain.

Mission accomplished

In this project, we assembled a fountain, a webserver framework, controlled the RGB LEDs, and set up e-mail alerts. They should look pretty according to the user's creativity.

Hotshot challenge

In this project, we set up e-mail alerts with the display. Is it possible to set Twitter alerts?

Project 6

Raspberry Pi as a Personal Assistant

In this project, we will build a tool using Raspberry Pi that acts as a personal assistant. This project presents ideas to overcome difficulties encountered in our day-to-day lives (for example, keeping track of daily appointments, paying bills on time), overcome procrastination, or ease our routine stress inducing activities by automating them.

Mission briefing

In this project, we build something that helps in simplifying our day-to-day activities, ease our burden in performing mundane tasks, and remind us about important appointments/ tasks as well as tracking them. We will work on implementing a solution for each possible scenario (for example, we will implement a solution to check e-mails and review a solution to create an alert for a new e-mail).

Why is it awesome?

We do our best to be successful in our career and lead a healthy lifestyle. While writing this book, we had to come up with a plan to overcome our procrastination and track our tasks effectively (especially, delivering the drafts of each project on time!).

Your objectives

In this project, we will accomplish the following:

- ▶ Setting up the e-mail feed parser
- ▶ Setting up the parser for reminders and events
- ▶ Designing an enclosure for the personal assistant
- ▶ Setting up the assembly for the dish monitor
- ▶ Setting up sensors for the key alert system

Mission checklist

In this task, we will work on installing all tools and Python modules used in this project:

1. Before we start installing the tools required for this project, if necessary, you can update the repositories and package lists as follows:

    ```
    sudo apt-get update
    ```

2. We will start with installing `python-feedparser`. We used the `python-feedparser` tool in the previous project and created e-mail alerts for the water fountain. If you skipped the previous project, the tool can be installed as follows:

    ```
    sudo apt-get install python-feedparser
    ```

3. We will use Google Calendar to organize events and appointments as an example. We need to install the `python-gdata` tool to make use of the Google APIs:

    ```
    sudo apt-get install python-gdata
    ```

4. Another important tool required for this project is OpenCV (`http://opencv.org/`). OpenCV is an open source computer vision framework developed by Intel. OpenCV is widely used by researchers and hobbyists in applications such as object recognition, machine vision applications such as component inspection on a manufacturing line, and more.

     It is important to know that it takes at least four hours to finish the compilation of OpenCV.

- The installation procedure for OpenCV on the Raspberry Pi has been borrowed from `http://mitchtech.net/raspberry-pi-opencv/` and the OpenCV installation guide for Linux (`http://docs.opencv.org/doc/tutorials/introduction/linux_install/linux_install.html`).

- Before we get started with the installation process, the dependencies for OpenCV need to be installed. The dependencies can be installed using the following shell script available along with this project:

```
sh OpenCVInstall.sh
```

- Once the dependencies have been installed, we can get started with the OpenCV installation. The source files to install OpenCV can be downloaded from `http://sourceforge.net/projects/opencvlibrary/files/opencv-unix/2.4.10/opencv-2.4.10.zip`.

- We need to extract the downloaded source:

```
unzip opencv-2.4.10.zip
```

- The next step is the makefile generation using **CMake**. The library has to be compiled with Python support that enables application development using a Python script library and support.

```
cd opencv-2.4.5
mkdir build
cd build
cmake -D CMAKE_BUILD_TYPE=RELEASE -D CMAKE_INSTALL_PREFIX=/
usr/local -D BUILD_NEW_PYTHON_SUPPORT=ON -D BUILD_
EXAMPLES=ON
```

- Once the makefile has been generated successfully, OpenCV can be built and installed as follows:

```
make
sudo make install
```

- Once the library has been installed, we need to test whether the installation was successful by executing one of the Python samples available in OpenCV:

```
cd ~/opencv-2.4.5/samples/python
python delaunay.py
```

❑   If the installation was successful, we should able to launch the Delaunay triangulation sample.

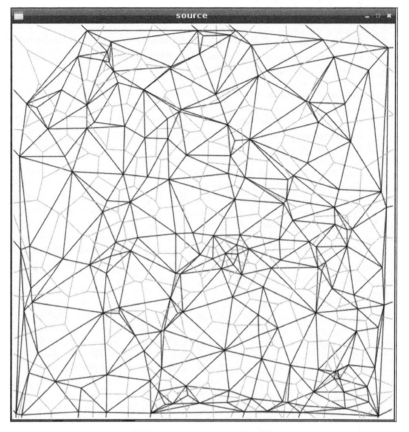

Delaunay triangulation – OpenCV

5.   Now that we have installed OpenCV, we will proceed to build our project over the forthcoming tasks of the project.

Setting up the e-mail feed parser

In this task, we will learn to set up an e-mail feed parser and blink an LED. As an example, we will check new e-mails in a Gmail account.

Prepare for lift off

Since we already installed the `python-feedparser` module, we will get started with setting up the mail parser. We will build each module of our project as a separate example.

Engage thrusters

1. Using Python IDLE, let's get started with writing a python script to achieve this task. We will get started by importing the `feedparser` module:

```
import sys
import feedparser
```

2. We will define the function required to check e-mails:

```
newEmail=""
username="username@gmail.com"
password="password"
proto="https://"
server="mail.google.com"
path="/gmail/feed/atom"
def mail():
  email = int(feedparser.parse(proto+username+":"+password+"@"+ser
ver+path)["feed"]["fullcount"])
  return email
```

 The preceding function has been borrowed from the WonderHowTo website (`http://null-byte.wonderhowto.com/how-to/make-gmail-notifier-python-0132845/`).

  - Let's save this function in a separate file and try to call it from another file. For example, the function has been saved in a file called `parser.py`.

  - We will import `parser.py` in another file as a module and implement the e-mail notifier. In this file, we will blink the LED when there is a new e-mail. We will start by importing the `parser` module and `RPi.GPIO`:

```
import parser
import time
import RPi.GPIO as gpio
```

  - We will get started by setting the output pins for the e-mail notifier example:

```
gpio.setwarnings(False)
gpio.setmode(gpio.BCM)
gpio.setup(17,gpio.OUT)
```

  - We will check for new e-mails and blink an LED if necessary:

```
while True:
  mail = parser.mail() #check for email
```

```
count = 0
if mail>0:                  #print for new emails
   print(mail)
   print("new emails \n")
   while count<10:
      count += 1
      gpio.output(17,gpio.HIGH) #blink LED if there are new
emails
      time.sleep(1)
      gpio.output(17,gpio.LOW)
      time.sleep(1)
   gpio.output(17,gpio.LOW) #set LED to low
else:
   time.sleep(10) #repeat cycle for 10 seconds
```

3. The LED needs to be connected as shown in the following diagram:

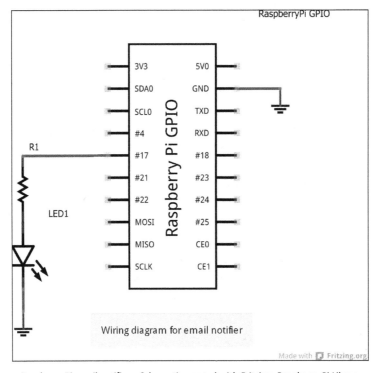

Wiring diagram for email notifier

Raspberry Pi email notifier – Schematic created with Fritzing, Raspberry Pi Library

Setting up the parser for reminders and events

In this task, we will implement a module that will blink an LED to remind us about important events and appointments.

Prepare for lift off

The Google Data Python client library is required for this task. You also have to save some tasks in your calendar to test the implementation.

Engage thrusters

1. Using the Python IDLE's editor, let's get started by creating a new file called `calendars.py`:

    ```
    import gdata.calendar.service
    import gdata.service
    import gdata.calendar
    import time
    ```

2. We can get started by defining a Google Calendar object. We will define the username and password for our Google account:

    ```
    calendar_service = gdata.calendar.service.CalendarService()
    calendar_service.email = 'username@gmail.com'
    calendar_service.password = 'password'
    calendar_service.ProgrammaticLogin()
    ```

3. The `calendar_query` function performs a query for calendar events by defining a time frame as follows:

    ```
    query = gdata.calendar.service.CalendarEventQuery('default','priva
    te','full')
    query.start_min = '2014-01-01'
    query.start_max = '2013-05-31'
    feed = calendar_service.CalendarQuery(query)
    return feed
    ```

4. Let's create another Python script and test the functionality of the calendar module (`calendar.py`). We will begin by importing the previous definition as a module:

    ```
    import calendar
      feed = calendar.calendar_query()
    ```

❑ Now, we will print the details of the retrieved events:

```
for i, an_event in enumerate(feed.entry):
  print '\t%s. %s' % (i, an_event.title.text,)
  for a_when in an_event.when:
    print '\t\tStart time: %s' % (a_when.start_time,)
    print '\t\tEnd time:   %s' % (a_when.end_time,)
```

❑ The preceding example was borrowed from the documentation of the Google Calendar API. When executed, the output would be something like the following:

```
0. Sai
    Start time: 2013-05-12T11:30:00.000-05:00
    End time:   2013-05-12T12:30:00.000-05:00
1. Event at Firegrill house
    Start time: 2013-04-24T18:30:00.000-05:00
    End time:   2013-04-24T19:30:00.000-05:00
2. Chicago Hardware Startup Meetup - FIRST MEETING
    Start time: 2013-01-23T18:30:00.000-06:00
    End time:   2013-01-23T21:00:00.000-06:00
3. Freescale SABRE Lite Board
    Start time: 2013-01-30T12:00:00.000-06:00
    End time:   2013-01-30T13:00:00.000-06:00
```

5. Since we are able to retrieve and parse the events on the Google Calendar, we will try to blink an LED to remind us about the events and appointments.

❑ We will get started with importing the `RPi.GPIO` module in the same file:

```
import calendar_special
import time
import datetime
import RPi.GPIO as gpio
```

❑ Since we used pin 17 for the e-mail alerts, let's use pin 24 for reminders and events.

❑ The events can be retrieved from Google Calendar as follows:

```
feed = calendar_special.calendar_query()   # retrieve events
from calendar
  for i, an_event in enumerate(feed.entry):
    for a_when in an_event.when: #We retrieve the start time
and end time for each appointment/event
      try:
        start_time = datetime.datetime.strptime(a_when.
start_time.split(".")[0], "%Y-%m-%dT%H:%M:%S")
```

```
          end_time = datetime.datetime.strptime(a_when.end_
time.split(".")[0], "%Y-%m-%dT%H:%M:%S")
        except ValueError:
        print(ValueError)
        continue
      current_time = datetime.datetime.now()
    if end_time > current_time: #Has the event ended?
      print '\t%s. %s' % (i, an_event.title.text,)
      print '\t\tStart time: %s' % (a_when.start_time,)
      print '\t\tEnd time:   %s' % (a_when.end_time,)
```

❑   We will filter out all upcoming events and list them with details. We will
    check whether we have set an alert for the event. If indeed there was an
    alert, we will blink an LED until the event has ended:

```
for reminder in a_when.reminder:
  if reminder.method == "alert" \
  and start_time - datetime.timedelta(0,60*int(reminder.
minutes))<current_time:
    print '\t%s. %s' % (i, an_event.title.text,)
    print '\t\tStart time: %s' % (a_when.start_time,)
    print '\t\tEnd time:   %s' % (a_when.end_time,)
    count = 0
    gpio.output(24,gpio.HIGH)
    time.sleep(1)
    gpio.output(24,gpio.LOW)
    time.sleep(1)
```

Designing an enclosure design for the personal assistant

In this task, we will look into the enclosure design for the project. In order to make things
simple, we will use a design that is open source. The enclosure is one that can be assembled
in few simple steps. This enclosure was designed by Michael Milazzo (http://makezine.
com/2013/01/18/laser-cutting-a-glueless-acrylic-project-box/).

Prepare for lift off

This enclosure can be fabricated in few simple steps using a laser cutter. The design available
along with this project in the PDF format can be modified using a design tool such as
Inkscape or Adobe Illustrator.

Engage thrusters

1. The enclosure design is meant to be manufactured using a laser cutter. Since laser cutters can be easily accessed from hackerspaces, open workshops, and so on, it should be easy to make this enclosure.

2. A laser cutter is easy to use when we adhere to safety practices. You must undergo training to operate a laser cutter. The files used for laser cutting are available from the preceding link.

3. Once the laser cutting operation is complete, the parts of the enclosure look like the one shown in the following image:

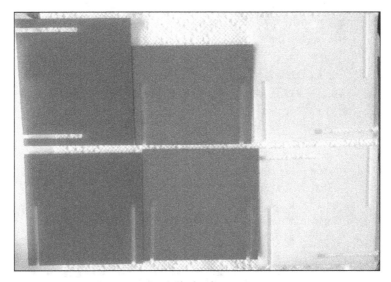

A Glueless box

4. The assembly of the enclosure is quite intuitive. We will make use of this enclosure in the later part of this project.

An assembled enclosure

Setting up the assembly for the dish monitor

In this task, we will set up a monitor over the kitchen sink. We will check whether there are dishes in the sink and send LED alerts to the user. Since we have installed OpenCV already, we will get started with the set up of the monitor.

This task was inspired by a hacker based in London who built a dish detector to alert users of a communal kitchen.

 The code sample for this function has been borrowed from the OpenCV Dish Detector project by Tom: `http://beagleboard.org/blog/2013-11-26-project-spotlight-dirty-dish-detector/`

Prepare for lift off

We will get started by mounting a camera on top of the sink and connecting it to an overhead camera, as shown in the following image:

An overhead camera on top of the sink

Engage thrusters

1. We will get started by importing the OpenCV module:

   ```
   import time
   import sys
   import cv2.cv as cv
   ```

2. We will initialize the camera to capture frames:

   ```
   capture = cv.CaptureFromCAM(0)
   ```

3. After initialization, we will grab a frame for processing:

   ```
   im = cv.QueryFrame(capture)
   ```

4. We'll convert the image to grayscale for image processing and feature detection:

   ```
   gray = cv.CreateImage(cv.GetSize(im),8,1)
   edges = cv.CreateImage(cv.GetSize(im),cv.IPL_DEPTH_8U,1)
   cv.CvtColor(im,gray,cv.CV_BGR2GRAY)
   ```

5. We will extract the features of the image using the **canny edge detection** technique. Since the information is prone to noise, we use the smoothing technique to eliminate the noise in the image:

```
cv.Canny(gray,edges,200,100,3)
cv.Smooth(gray,gray,cv.CV_GAUSSIAN,3,3)
```

6. We will attempt to detect the dishes using common shapes found in the dishes. The technique is called **Hough transforms** and we will try to detect circular objects in the image:

```
storage = cv.CreateMat(640,1,cv.CV_32FC3)
cv.HoughCircles(gray,storage,cv.CV_HOUGH_GRADIENT,1,30,100,55,0,0)
```

7. We will draw a circle around each object detected. This helps in eliminating any incorrect object detection:

```
for i in range(storage.rows ):
  val = storage[i, 0]
  vessels = vessels + 1 #increment dishes detected by 1
  radius = int(val[2])
  center = (int(val[0]), int(val[1]))
  cv.Circle(im, center, radius, (0, 0, 255), 3, 8, 0)
```

8. The objects detected can be viewed as follows:

Dishes detected in OpenCV

9. If a vessel is detected, we will trigger an LED alert to annoy the user.

Objective complete – mini debriefing

We have set up a dish monitor to alert the user when dishes are detected using an LED.

Setting up sensors for the key alert system

In this task, we will try to build a module that tries to alert the user if the things that we use daily (such as the keys to our apartment door or the car key) are not found in the right place. It helps us save a lot of time frantically searching for misplaced items. We will use a reed switch and a magnet for this module.

The uniqueness about this task is that we try to improve our lives with simple items that are easy to purchase and simple to build. A magnet and a reed switch are available from all hobby stores. You can also use a reed switch in door security systems. The following is a diagram of a reed switch interfaced to a Raspberry Pi:

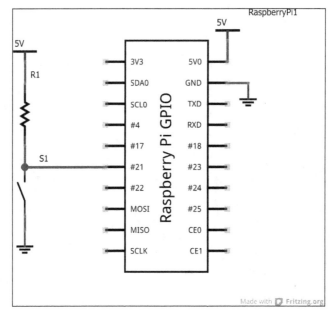

Reed switch setup with the Raspberry Pi GPIO

Prepare for lift off

We will interface the reed switch as shown in the preceding diagram. Let's test it on a breadboard before setting it up in an enclosure:

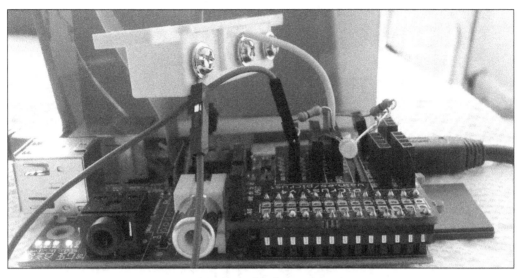

Reed switch interfaced to Raspberry Pi

Engage thrusters

1. We will be tracking whether the key is in the right place by attaching a bar magnet to the keys. We will set up a GPIO pin as we get started:

    ```
    import RPi.GPIO as GPIO
    GPIO.setmode(GPIO.BCM)
    GPIO.setwarnings(False)
    GPIO.setmode(GPIO.BCM)
    GPIO.setup(18,GPIO.IN)
    ```

2. We will read the inputs and if the magnet in the key is not nearby the reed switch, we should be able to trigger an alert:

    ```
    while True:
      if(GPIO.input(18)):
        print("Keys are in the right place")
      else
        print("Keys missing!")
    ```

3. Now that we have set an input for the reed switch, we should be able to set up the reed switch inside the enclosure as shown in the following image:

A reed switch with the magnet attached to the key

Objective complete – mini debriefing

In this task, you learned to use a simple reed switch to the Raspberry Pi and help improve our lives.

Mission accomplished

In this project we implemented different modules, including e-mail alerts, calendar alerts, a dish monitor, and a key alert system. We leave it to the user to integrate all subsystems using their creativity. You (like us) have learned to use Raspberry Pi to improve our quality of life.

Hotshot challenges

How can we use Raspberry Pi to enhance the lives of senior citizens?

The dish detector is noise prone. How can it be improved?

References

1. *OpenCV installation on the Raspberry Pi* available at `http://mitchtech.net/raspberry-pi-opencv/`.

2. *OpenCV guide for installation on Ubuntu* available at `http://docs.opencv.org/doc/tutorials/introduction/linux_install/linux_install.html`.

3. *Python Gmail notifier* from the *WonderHowTo* website, `http://null-byte.wonderhowto.com/how-to/make-gmail-notifier-python-0132845/`.

4. *Google data client API documentation* for *Google Calendar*.

5. *Google Calendar using pynotify* by *Julien Danjou*.

6. *OpenCV dish detector*, available at, `http://www.adafruit.com/blog/2014/03/11/beaglebone-black-used-to-detect-dirty-dishes-beagleboneblack-txinstruments-beagleboardorg/`, *Tom, London hackerspace*.

Project 7

Raspberry Pi-based Line Following Robot

In this project, we will build a line following robot that is controlled by your Raspberry Pi.

It is absolutely not necessary to make use of the Raspberry Pi to build a line following robot unless you are using a camera to follow the line. We are building this robot to demonstrate an example of building a mechatronic system using the Raspberry Pi.

Mission briefing

In this project, we will build a line following robot that will follow a black line against a white background. The robot will make use of a pair of infrared sensors to track the orientation of the robot and drive the robot accordingly.

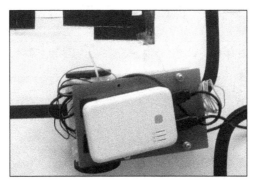

A line following robot

Why is it awesome?

The Pi, as you have seen in the last few projects, offers you immense functionality and many advantages over microcontrollers. You can bring this power and smaller footprints to robotics. So, we are getting you started off with the line following robot. Once you get this under control, the possibilities are endless, making this an awesome segue into robotics and beyond.

Your Hotshot objectives

In this project, we will build the line following robot in the following steps:

- ▶ Assembly of the Pi Plate for the line following robot
- ▶ Sensor selection, interfacing sensors, and data interpretation
- ▶ Implementation of line following logic based on sensor data
- ▶ Testing the motor driver circuit
- ▶ Preparation of the line following course
- ▶ Designing the chassis for the line following robot
- ▶ A step-by-step assembly of the robot

Mission checklist

There are off-the-shelf products available to build a line following robot, for example, **Make:it Basic Robotics Starter Kit** (http://www.makershed.com/products/makeit-robotics-start-kit). Alternatively, in order to build a line following robot, the following items are required and the reader may add or remove components to the robot based on his/her creativity:

Item	Cost
A line following sensor array	10 USD (in terms of components)
DC motors with a gearbox * 2 – 60 rpm (http://www.pololu.com/product/1594)	11 USD
Arduino Uno (http://store.arduino.cc/product/A000066)	30 USD
Plastic wheels – 1 pair (http://www.pololu.com/product/1425)	8 USD

Item	Cost
H Bridge chip – for example, L293D (`http://www.pololu.com/product/24`)	3 USD
An acrylic sheet (preferably 12 inch x 24 inch to cut the chassis using a laser cutter)	5 USD
A USB battery pack (preferably 10,000 mAh, 1A max output)	15 USD
A poster board	3 USD
Pi Plate from Adafruit Industries (`https://www.adafruit.com/product/801`)	15 USD

Assembly of the Pi Plate for the line following robot

 The Pi Plate is necessary only if you are going to build your own circuitry (instead of an off-the-shelf robot kit) that drives the robot.

We will make use of the Pi Plate from Adafruit Industries. The Pi Plate is stackable and an add-on hardware for the Raspberry Pi. The Pi Plate is like a breadboard/perforated prototyping board and enables prototyping using the Raspberry Pi platform. We will assemble the headers on the board.

Prepare for lift off

The Pi Plate is available from Adafruit Industries (`www.adafruit.com`). It costs 15.95 USD. This stackable add-on hardware is useful because the sensors and actuators can be connected using the screw-in terminals. This will avoid any loose connections to your Raspberry Pi while the robot is in motion.

Engage thrusters

1. The contents of the Pi Plate package are as follows:

Contents of a Pi Plate package

 Adult supervision is required for soldering and putting the Pi Plate together.

2. The Pi Plate requires soldering of the terminals, and Adafruit has some tutorials in setting up the Pi Plate. When the terminals and headers are assembled together, we have what is shown in the following image:

A Pi Plate stacked on the Raspberry Pi

Objective complete – mini debriefing

It is unlikely that there will be a problem with the Pi Plate unless there is a cold solder.

Sensor selection, interface, and data interpretation

In this task, we will discuss the different sensors available to build a line following robot and pick a sensor for this project.

Engage thrusters

We will discuss three sensors in this task, including light detecting resistors, IR emitters/detectors, and a camera. We will discuss their operations, features, and their distinct edge over other sensing techniques as well as their disadvantages.

Light Dependent Resistors

As the name suggests, Light Dependent Resistors are those that change their resistance when light is incident on the surface of the resistor.

Light Dependent Resistors are used in combination with a bright LED. We can make use of the difference in reflectivity between different coloured surfaces to follow a black line on a dark surface.

When Light Dependent Resistor is inserted into a potential divider configuration, as shown in the following diagram, the drop in voltage causes a potential imbalance leading to a change in voltage. Since the reflectance of white and black color surfaces varies, the change in voltage can be used to distinguish between black and white colors. This property of Light Dependent Resistors can be used in our line following robot:

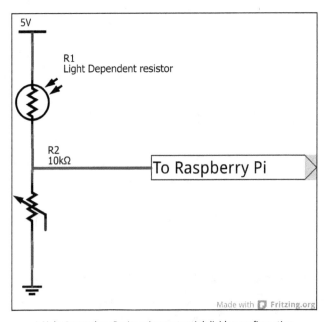

A Light Dependant Resistor in a potential divider configuration

The potentiometer in the potential divider configuration is used to adjust the sensitivity of Light Dependent Resistors depending upon the surrounding lighting conditions.

Light Dependent Resistors can be used as a sensor to build a line following robot, except in those cases where the sensor response time is not trivial. Hence, LDRs cannot be used in cases where the robot is designed to move at higher speeds.

Light Dependent Resistors have to be completely isolated from light sources other than the bright white LED. This is to make sure that the LED responds to reflected light from the bright LED.

Infrared emitter/detector

An infrared (IR) emitter/detector combination is the best alternative to the Light Dependent Resistors. In both cases (the LDR and IR sensors), the emitter (ultra bright white LED/IR LED) and the detector (Light Dependent Resistors or photodiode) are arranged next to each other.

The following diagram shows the circuit for an IR emitter/detector:

An IR emitter/detector for the line following robot

The preceding figure shows a photodiode that is connected to the inverting terminal of an op-amp. The potentiometer (that is connected to the non-inverting terminal of the op-amp) can be used to vary the sensitivity of the sensor.

When light falls on the photodiode, it pulls down the 10K resistor, and hence, the output of the op-amp is high. The signal diode, 1N4148, acts as a signal level converter between 5V and 3.3V (Raspberry Pi's GPIO pins are 3.3V tolerant). When the 5V side is high, the 3.3V side is also high (the diode is reverse biased and hence the pull up resistor keeps the 3.3V side high). When the infrared sensor is on top of the black surface, the output of the op-amp is low (since the inverting terminal is high) and the pull up resistor on the 3.3V side is pulled down. Thus, the GPIO pin is pulled down. The infrared sensor shown in the preceding diagram can only be used in controlled lighting conditions as they are prone to stray infrared radiation from daylight.

In conditions where the robot has to operate under broad daylight conditions, the infrared transmitter and receiver has to be pulse width modulated so that the sensor can distinguish between noise and the actual signal (more information can be found at http://www.ermicro.com/blog/?p=1908).

Machine-vision-based line following robot

The final alternative to a sensor to build a line following robot is a camera. The Raspberry Pi foundation has released its own camera module and it is also simple to interface.

A line following robot can be implemented by grabbing a frame from the camera module and converting it into a grayscale image. The grayscale image can be used to determine the current position of the robot with respect to the line that has to be followed. Since white and grey surfaces have varying levels of grey colour, the orientation of the robot can be corrected using a differential steering mechanism.

A camera would be overkill for building a line following robot to just follow a black line on a white surface in an indoor environment (also, a bit overwhelming for a beginner). However, we can use it out of an academic interest.

Sensor selection

We have discussed the different sensing options available for building a line following robot. We will choose the infrared sensor. We chose the infrared sensor for the following reasons:

- ▶ It can be used only in controlled lighting conditions (since we are using an unmodulated infrared light source) but serves as a good start for a beginner
- ▶ It is readily available and easy to interface
- ▶ It has a distinct edge over light detecting resistors since it has a better response time

Objective complete – mission debriefing

In this task, we discussed the different sensor options available for a line following robot.

Implementation of line following logic based on sensor data

In this task, we will implement a simple line following technique using the infrared sensor. We will make use of a pair of infrared sensors to track a black line on a white surface. The robot will move forward if both the sensors are on a white surface. The robot turns left if the left sensor is on the black line and vice versa.

Prepare for lift off

The sensor needs to be soldered and connected to the Raspberry Pi (something like the one shown in the preceding schematic). Alternatively, you may use a sensor of your choice.

Engage thrusters

1. As always, we will get started by importing the required modules, especially `Rpi.GPIO`:

```
import RPi.GPIO as GPIO
from time import sleep
```

2. We will set the pin configuration that we will use in this program:

```
GPIO.setwarnings(False)
GPIO.setmode(GPIO.BCM)
GPIO.setup(18,GPIO.IN)
GPIO.setup(25,GPIO.IN)
```

3. The control logic explained earlier is implemented as follows:

```
state = 1
prev_state = 0
while True:
   #both sensors are on white surface
   if ((GPIO.input(18)==GPIO.HIGH) and (GPIO.input(25)==GPIO.HIGH)):
      state = 0
   #left sensor alone is on the black surface
   elif ((GPIO.input(18)==GPIO.LOW) and (GPIO.input(25)==GPIO.HIGH)):
      state = 1
   #right sensor alone is on the black surface
   elif ((GPIO.input(18)==GPIO.HIGH) and (GPIO.input(25)==GPIO.LOW)):
      state = 2
   #if sensor state has changed since last time, update motor control
   if state != prev_state:
     if state == 0:
       #move robot forward
     elif state == 1:
       #turn robot left
     elif state == 2:
       #turn robot right
     prev_state = state

   sleep(0.15)
```

The sensor states are checked once every 15 milliseconds. If there is a change of sensor states, the motor control is updated (as per the logic explained in this task).

4. Since we are using only two sensors, the robot runs crisscross across the line. In order to achieve smooth tracking of the line, a sensor array is used for driving the motors using a control algorithm such as a PID control algorithm.

Objective complete – mini debriefing

In this task, we implemented the line following logic for our robot. In the next task, we will discuss motor control to drive the robot This would be eventually integrated into the line following logic.

Testing the motor driver circuit

In this project, we will use a pair of DC motors to drive the robot. We will use a dual H-bridge (SN754410) driver to control the DC motors. We will use a software PWM library written for the Raspberry Pi. We chose DC motors for the following reasons:

1. DC motors are easy to operate and control using an H-bridge interfaced to the Raspberry Pi.

2. There is a software PWM library that makes it easier to control the DC motors.

In this task, we will implement the DC motor control circuit and also write a program to control the DC motors.

Prepare for lift off

We will use the software PWM function available with `RPi.GPIO`. The software PWM function is available on versions greater than 0.5.3. We need to determine the `RPi.GPIO` version installed on the Raspberry Pi using a command-line terminal:

```
python
import RPi.GPIO
RPi.GPIO.VERSION
```

If the returned value is earlier than 0.53, the package can be updated as follows:

```
sudo apt-get update
sudo apt-get upgrade
```

We will be making use of pulse width modulation to drive the DC motors. It is important that you familiarize yourself with pulse width modulation techniques to control a DC motor. We also need to set up the DC motors for testing by connecting the wheels to the motor (something similar to the following figure):

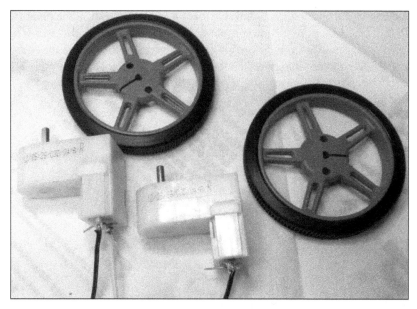

DC motors with soldered wires and wheels with strapped silicone tires

We also need to construct the motor control circuitry as shown in the following schematic:

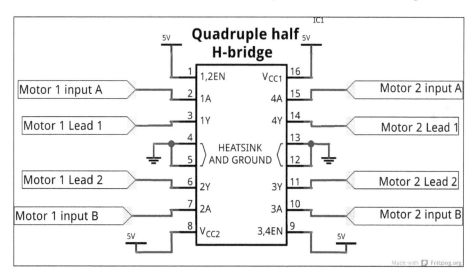

A SN754410 motor control circuitry

An H-bridge circuit is used for bidirectional control of a DC motor using a microcontroller or Raspberry Pi (`https://itp.nyu.edu/physcomp/labs/motors-and-transistors/dc-motor-control-using-an-h-bridge/`). The H-Bridge takes in 2 inputs for each motor. The following table shows a logic table that dictates the control of a motor using an H-Bridge:

FUNCTION TABLE (each driver)		
INPUTS†		OUTPUT
A	EN	Y
H	H	H
L	H	L
X	L	Z

H = high-level, L = low-level
X = irrelevant
Z = high-impedance (off)
† In the thermal shutdown mode, the output is in a high-impedance state regardless of the input levels.

The SN754410 truth table

For example, if pin 1A is set to high while 2A is set to low and the leads of the motor are connected to 1Y and 2Y respectively, the motor rotates in one direction, while it rotates in the opposite direction when 1A is set to low and 2A is set to high.

Engage thrusters

1. We will get started with the testing of the DC motors with a simple Python program. We will get started by importing the modules:

```
import RPi.GPIO as GPIO
import time
```

2. We will declare the pins that will be used as output pins. We will connect the GPIO pins, 8, 9, 10, and, 11 to motor driver pins, 1A, 2A, 3A, and 4A, respectively:

```
GPIO.setwarning(False)
GPIO.setmode(GPIO.BCM)

GPIO.setup(8,GPIO.OUT)  #connected to 1A
GPIO.setup(9,GPIO.OUT)  #connected to 2A
GPIO.setup(10,GPIO.OUT)  #connected to 3A
GPIO.setup(11,GPIO.OUT)  #connected to 4A
```

3. We test both the motors by rotating them in both directions for 10 seconds and stopping them:

```
while True:
#Rotate both motors forward for 10 seconds
GPIO.output(8,GPIO.HIGH)
GPIO.output(9,GPIO.LOW)

GPIO.output(10,GPIO.HIGH)
GPIO.output(11,GPIO.LOW)
sleep(10)
#Stop motors and rotate in reverse directions
GPIO.output(8,GPIO.LOW)
GPIO.output(10,GPIO.LOW)
#Go reverse
GPIO.output(9,GPIO.HIGH)
GPIO.output(11,GPIO.HIGH)
sleep(10)
#Stop motors and rotate both in opposite directions
GPIO.output(9,GPIO.LOW)
GPIO.output(11,GPIO.LOW)

GPIO.output(8,GPIO.HIGH)
GPIO.output(9,GPIO.LOW)

GPIO.output(10,GPIO.LOW)
GPIO.output(11,GPIO.HIGH)
sleep(10)
#Stop Motors
GPIO.output(8,GPIO.LOW)
GPIO.output(9,GPIO.LOW)
GPIO.output(10,GPIO.LOW)
GPIO.output(11,GPIO.LOW)
```

4. In the preceding example, both the motors were running at 100 percent duty cycle. We will look into controlling the motors using pulse width modulation. We will set the pins as output and declare the operating channel frequencies for the PWM pins (1kHz):

```
GPIO.setup(8,GPIO.OUT) #connected to 1A
GPIO.setup(9,GPIO.OUT) #connected to 2A
GPIO.setup(10,GPIO.OUT) #connected to 3A
GPIO.setup(11,GPIO.OUT) #connected to 4A

GPIO.output(9,GPIO.HIGH)
```

```
GPIO.output(11,GPIO.HIGH)

motor1 = GPIO.PWM(8,1000)
motor2 = GPIO.PWM(10,1000)
```

5. We will start the pulse width modulation signal (10 percent duty cycle – runs at 10 percent of the rated voltage) as follows:

```
motor1.start(10)
motor2.start(10)
```

❑ We can vary the speed of the motor as follows:

```
while True:
motor1.ChangeDutyCycle(25)
motor2.ChangeDutyCycle(25)
sleep(15)
motor1.ChangeDutyCycle(50)
motor2.ChangeDutyCycle(50)
sleep(15)
motor1.ChangeDutyCycle(75)
motor2.ChangeDutyCycle(75)
sleep(15)
motor1.ChangeDutyCycle(100)
motor2.ChangeDutyCycle(100)
sleep(15)
```

Objective complete – mini debriefing

In this task, we implemented a motor driver circuitry and tested it.

Preparation of the line following course

In this task, we will prepare the line following track for the robot.

Prepare for lift off

There are two approaches to building a line following track. They include the following:

1. Print a track available from **Parallax** and set it on top of a posterboard.

2. Use electrical tape and build a track using a tutorial from **Pololu**.

The following items are required to complete this task:

1. A posterboard

2. A permanent marker

3. A pencil

4. A ruler

5. A4 sheets

Engage thrusters

1. We will use a readily available line for the following track (`http://www.parallax.com/sites/default/files/downloads/28136-S2-PrintableTracks.pdf`) designed for the **Scribbler** line following robot from Parallax. The line following track from Parallax consists of 10 individual pieces of track that can be arranged and customized according to our needs.

2. We will get started with printing two sets of the track available along with this project's downloads and arrange them according to our needs and determine the complicity of the track. An example of the track is shown in the following image, and this can be considered the fastest way of building a line following track:

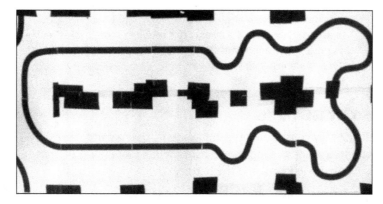

A line following track

Use electrical tape and build a track

Pololu has published an excellent tutorial (`https://www.pololu.com/docs/pdf/0J22/building_line_courses.pdf`) on building a track using electrical tape. The only disadvantage behind using this method to build a track is that the wrinkles on the electrical tape can affect the smooth operation of the robot.

Designing the chassis for the line following robot

In this task, we will design the chassis for the line following robot. There are several options available in terms of design tools for the design of the chassis. We chose *Autodesk Inventor*, but there are a lot of tools such as Autodesk 123D and so on.

Prepare for lift off

The chassis for the robot is fabricated using the laser cutting technique. You are welcome to fabricate your own chassis. We have chosen to use laser cutting because it is the easiest to complete. The technique involves designing the chassis followed by preparing the design for fabrication and laser cutting.

You may download the design file available along with this project and use it for laser cutting. There is a trial version of **Autodesk Inventor** available for download and it can be installed and used for designing a custom chassis.

As a maker/hacker, it is important that you learn how to use these tools and how to design a chassis.

The use of tools such as a laser cutter requires some basic training and supervision. It is important that you undergo the requisite safety training before operating such equipment.

Engage thrusters

1. We will begin by considering the components that go into the robot. The components include the infrared sensors, a ball caster, two DC motors, the Raspberry Pi, the Pi Plate, and the battery.

2. Since the Pi Plate will be stacked on top of the Raspberry Pi, we will mount the battery on a separate plate mounted on top of the Raspberry Pi. The component positions are designed based on intuition. The chassis is shown in the following image:

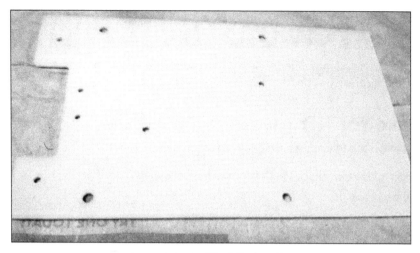

Laser cut chassis of line following robot

3. The top plate that holds the battery pack is shown in the following image:

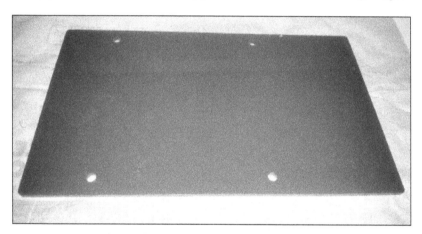

A top plate used to mount the battery of the line following robot

Objective complete – mini debriefing

We have finished designing the parts and fabricating them using a laser cutter.

A step-by-step assembly of the robot

In this task, we will assemble the robot in simple steps that are accompanied by a photographical representation.

Prepare for lift off

We need to have the following parts ready to assemble the robot:

1. Top and bottom chassis plates for the line following robot
2. Infrared sensors
3. A pair of #2 screws and nuts (washers optional)
4. A ball caster assembly with screws from *Pololu*
5. 2*M2.5 screws for mounting the Raspberry Pi (washers optional)
6. 4*#6 1-inch screws with spacers (washers optional)
7. A Raspberry Pi
8. Velcro
9. Battery
10. 2 DC motors
11. Double-sided tape
12. A Pi Plate
13. A motor driver

Engage thrusters

1. We will get started by mounting the castor wheel.

Mounting the castor wheel

2. We will mount the Raspberry Pi using M2.5 screws.

Raspberry Pi mounted using M2.5 screws

3. This is followed by the DC motors coupled with wheels using the double-sided tape. The DC motors with a plastic gearbox from Pololu do not come with a mounting hole, and hence, we will use double-sided tape to mount the motors. Similarly, the infrared sensors were also mounted using double-sided tape at the center with a spacing that is half the width of the track.

DC motors mounted using double-sided tape

4. We will mount the Pi Plate and the top chassis plate. We will use velcro to mount the USB battery pack to complete the line following robot assembly.

An assembled robot

5. Once the assembly is completed, we have to connect the motors and the sensors to get started with the testing.

Objective complete – mini debriefing

We have completed the assembly of the line following robot in this task. Once the motor control code is implemented into the line following logic, we are all set to testing the robot on the track. This may require some tweaking the motor speed to make the robot track the line effectively.

Mission accomplished

In this project, we built a line following robot step by step. We got started with the sensors followed by motor control, chassis design, arena design, and integration. Now, we have a line following robot.

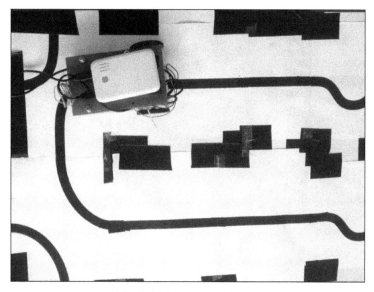

A line following robot on the arena

Hotshot challenge

In this project, we did not make use of any motor control algorithm (like PID) to steer the robot. How do we implement one?

References

The Pololu tutorial on *Building Line Following and Line Maze Courses* can be found at `http://www.pololu.com/docs/0J22`

The *Advanced Line Following with 3pi: PID Control* tutorial can be found at `http://www.pololu.com/docs/0J21/7.c`

The Parallax line following track: `http://www.parallax.com/Portals/0/Downloads/docs/prod/robo/scribbler2/Tracks.pdf`

Project 8

Connect Four Desktop Game using Raspberry Pi

In this project, we will build a desktop game enabled by the Raspberry Pi. We will build a prototype using a cardboard box, a monitor, and an input control on the cabinet and implement optional speakers and a marquee for the game. The game will make use of the `python-pygame` module (a game engine available under GPL license: `http://pygame.org/wiki/about`).

Mission briefing

A **Connect Four** game is a two-player game where the objective is to connect four coins of the same color in a vertical, horizontal, or diagonal fashion (more information is available at `http://en.wikipedia.org/wiki/Connect_Four`). We will install the necessary software packages and add all the necessary accessories to make a desktop prototype. The Connect Four game in this project is based on the book *Making Games with Python & Pygame* (`http://inventwithpython.com/makinggames.pdf`). This desktop game is a great start for people who are trying to getting started with electronics as a hobby.

When we finish this project, our cabinet will be something like the one shown in the following image:

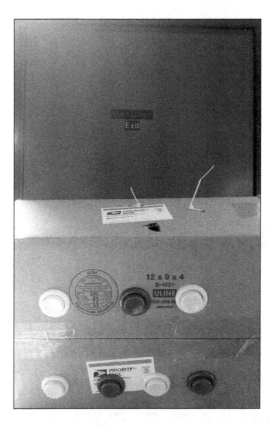

Why is it awesome?

If you are like us and have ever visited the arcade and wondered how much fun it will be to build a game yourself, this project is for you. Single board computers such as Raspberry Pi and sites such as **Instructables** (http://www.instructables.com/) only make things easier, and of course, isn't it fun to consider adapting the design and leave your own stamp on it? We will focus on the Pi and how to use it for the game and leave the rest up to what you find on the Internet and your own imagination.

In this project, we will present the subsystems of what could possibly go into building a mini desktop/tabletop arcade such as a game using Raspberry Pi. We will not concentrate on presenting a better user interface for the game or a cabinet, but rather what it takes to build something similar to an arcade game, including game launch, hardware interface, and so on.

Your objectives

We will build our Connect Four desktop game through the following activities:

> ▸ Installation of the pre-requisites (*Mission checklist*)
>
> ▸ A hello world example with the `Python-pygame`
>
> ▸ Input control design for the game
>
> ▸ Getting started with the Connect Four game (UI + sound effects)
>
> ▸ A brief description of the Connect Four Game AI
>
> ▸ Marquee design and control
>
> ▸ Setting up of the switches using a cardboard box

Mission checklist

One of the main prerequisites for this project is the installation of `Python-pygame`. The tool can be installed in a single step as follows:

```
sudo apt-get install python-pygame
```

This is the only software tool that we will use in this project. We require the following items for the construction of the arcade cabinet. We also need the following items for the project:

Item	Estimated Cost
A cardboard box	
Momentary Press buttons – Arcade style * 8 (`http://na.suzohapp.com/all_catalogs/pushbuttons/58-9111-L`)	2.70 USD each
16*32 LED display from Adafruit or Pi-Lite display for the Raspberry Pi (optional)	USD 40 USD /31 USD
A monitor of the reader's choice with signal cable to connect to Raspberry Pi	50 USD approximately
Raspberry Pi	25 USD/35 USD
RGB LED strip (optional)	10 USD approximately

Hello world example with the pygame

In this task, we will learn the usage of `pygame` for game development. We will get started with an example that opens a blank window and write a couple of lines to monitor events so that we can quit the program if the window is closed.

We will go through the important features of the `pygame` module, which is necessary to build our arcade game, including playing sounds and controlling the menu.

Prepare for lift off

As mentioned earlier, this project is based on the book *Making Games with Python & Pygame* (http://inventwithpython.com/makinggames.pdf). In this task, we will go through select features of the `pygame` module. It is important that you familiarize yourself with the different features available under the `pygame` module.

Engage thrusters

1. We will get started by importing the modules required for the *Hello world* example. We will import the `pygame` and the `sys` module:

   ```
   import pygame,sys
   ```

2. Next, we will also import `pygame.locals`, since it contains several constant variables:

   ```
   from pygame.locals import *
   ```

3. In order to make use of the functions of the `pygame` module, we need to initialize the module:

   ```
   pygame.init()
   ```

4. We will set the window width and height parameters and create a `pygame.Surface` object that is stored in a variable called `DISPLAYSURF`:

   ```
   DISPLAYSURF = pygame.display.set_mode((400, 300))
   ```

5. We will set the window title name:

   ```
   pygame.display.set_caption('Hello World!')
   ```

6. Now, we will run a loop that waits for events inside the window and update the display through every cycle. In this example, we do not have anything to be updated. We will quit the program when the user closes the window:

   ```
   while True: # main game loop
     for event in pygame.event.get():
       if event.type == QUIT:
         pygame.quit()
         sys.exit()

     pygame.display.update()
   ```

7. This should open up a blank window titled **Hello World**.

Playing sounds using the pygame module

Since the sound effects form the crux of an arcade game, we need to know how to play sounds using the pygame platform.

1. We will declare a sound object to play the beeps.wav file, available along with the downloads of this file. The file needs to be copied into the same directory as the python script that runs the game as follows:

    ```
    soundObj = pygame.mixer.Sound('beeps.wav')
    ```

2. The sound can be played in a loop by calling the play() method as follows:

    ```
    while True: # main game loop
       soundObj.play()
    ```

3. We can stop playing the sound file by calling the stop() method.

Building menus using the pygame module

1. We will need a simple menu for our desktop game. We will make use of the *menu class* (distributed under GNU GPL v3 license) written by *Scott Barlow*. Let's review the simple_example.py example. (http://www.pygame.org/project-MenuClass-1260-.html.)

2. In this menu example, a menu object is created; when a menu option is selected using a keyboard, the selected option is highlighted and printed on a terminal when the return key is pressed. For example, when the down key is pressed to select **Load Game** and the return key pressed, the Load Game option is printed to the terminal.

3. Let's discuss the parameters that need to be passed as arguments to create a menu object. According to the documentation available with the menu class, a menu object has to be defined with the following parameters:

    ```
    menu = cMenu(x, y, h_pad, v_pad, orientation, number,
    background,buttonList)
    ```

    *   The parameters x and y refer to the location of the origin of the menu object on the game screen

    *   The parameters h_pad and v_pad refer to the spacing between the buttons in the horizontal and vertical directions

    *   The orientation parameter refers to the arrangement of the buttons on the screen, that is, 'horizontal' or 'vertical'

    *   The number parameter refers to the number of buttons that can be accommodated in a single row (when arranged horizontally) or in a single column (when arranged vertically)

❑ The `background` parameter refers to the surface on which the menu has to be created

❑ The `buttonList` parameter refers to the list of buttons that we want on the screen

4. We will get started by declaring a menu object and listing all the options we want in the menu, namely:

```
menu = cMenu(50, 50, 20, 5, 'vertical', 100, screen,
  [('Start Game', 1, None),
  ('Score Board', 2, None),
  ('Exit', 3, None)])
```

5. The menu needs to be centered on the surface of the screen:

```
menu.set_center(True, True)
```

6. The text of the menu buttons also needs to be aligned:

```
menu.set_alignment('center', 'center')
```

7. In order to display and update the menu and selection parameters, a simple state machine is used:

```
state = 0
prev_state = 1
```

8. The `pygame.event.wait()` method detects any keyboard or mouse events and updates the current state accordingly.

9. The menu is updated by the method (due to a key press event / return key press):

```
pygame.event.post(pygame.event.Event(EVENT_CHANGE_STATE,
key = 0))
```

10. When the return key is pressed to select an option, the selected option is printed to the terminal and the menu is updated by highlighting the selected option (in red) by

```
rect_list, state = menu.update(e, state):

while True:
  if prev_state != state:
    pygame.event.post(pygame.event.Event
(EVENT_CHANGE_STATE, key = 0))
    prev_state = state

  e = pygame.event.wait()

  if e.type == pygame.KEYDOWN or e.type == EVENT_CHANGE_STATE:
    if state == 0:
      rect_list, state = menu.update(e, state)
```

```
      elif state == 1:
        print 'Start Game!'
        state = 0
      elif state == 2:
        print 'Load Game!'
        state = 0
      elif state == 3:
        print 'Options!'
        state = 0
      else:
        print 'Exit!'
        pygame.quit()
        sys.exit()
  # Quit if the user presses the exit button
  if e.type == pygame.QUIT:
    pygame.quit()
    sys.exit()

  # Update the screen
  pygame.display.update()
```

Objective complete – mini debriefing

We have finished testing the `pygame` module and reviewed a simple menu design example along with testing the playing of sounds using the `pygame` module.

Getting started with the Connect Four game (UI and sound effects)

In this task, we will work on some preliminary tweaks for the Connect Four game. We will take the example from *New Game Source Code: Four in a Row*, `http://inventwithpython.com/blog/2011/06/10/new-game-source-code-four-in-a-row/`, and make use of the examples discussed in the previous task, namely, playing sounds and menu design and add them to the Connect Four Game Python script.

Prepare for lift off

We need the Connect Four game example (four in a row example—`fourinarow.py`) from the book. The example can be downloaded from `http://invpy.com/fourinarowimages.zip`.

Engage Thrusters

1. In this project, the game needs to be launched fullscreen as soon as Raspberry Pi (that has been set up to launch the desktop game) is powered up.

2. The `pygame.display.set_mode` method is used to set the game to fullscreen with the `pygame.FULLSCREEN` argument. The resolution of the game will be (*Window width x Window height*), in this case, 640 x 480 pixels:

   ```
   DISPLAYSURF = pygame.display.set_mode((WINDOWWIDTH,
   WINDOWHEIGHT),pygame.FULLSCREEN)
   ```

3. In order to launch the game (the Python script: `Connect_four.py`) after Raspberry Pi is powered up, let's create a shell script using a text editor with the following contents and call it `startup.sh`:

   ```
   #!/bin/sh

   python Connect_four.py
   ```

4. The shell script needs to be saved to the `/home/pi` location. Alternatively, the script can be saved at any other location.

5. The shell script has to be made an executable file using the `chmod` command:

   `sudo chmod 755 startup.sh`

6. In order to execute `startup.sh` upon boot, the `/etc/rc.local` file needs to be modified. In the command-line terminal of Raspberry Pi, the file can be opened using a text editor such as `nano`:

   ```
   sudo nano /etc/rc.local
   ```

7. Before the last line of the file, `exit 0`, the following lines have to be added:

   ```
   sleep 10
   cd /home/pi/
   /home/pi/startup.sh &
   exit 0
   ```

8. The script is executed after all the kernel modules are initialized. The script is executed from the directory where the files have been saved.

Adding a menu for the game

The next step is to add a menu for the game. As discussed in the previous task, we will make of the *menu class* available at `http://www.pygame.org/project-MenuClass-1260-.html`

1. The first step is to import the menu class into the Connect Four game's Python script:

    ```
    from menu import *
    ```

2. Let's create a menu object with the `Start Game` options to launch the game and `Exit` to quit the game. We will integrate the menu from the first task of this project. We will get started by adding the menu that needs to be drawn on the surface:

    ```
    menu = cMenu(50,50,20,5,'vertical',100, DISPLAYSURF,
       [('Start Game' ,1,None),
       ('Exit' ,2,None)])
    ```

3. Let's set the background of the menu to a blue color:

    ```
    DISPLAYSURF.fill(BGCOLOR)
    ```

4. Using the menu design discussed in the previous task, let's add a line to launch the game when the **Start Game** option is selected. The game is launched by calling the `runGame(isFirstGame)` method:

    ```
    if state == 0:
      rect_list,state = menu.update(e,state)
    elif state == 1:
      runGame(isFirstGame)
      isFirstGame = False
      state = 0
    elif state == 2 :
      print 'Exit'
      pygame.quit()
      sys.exit()
      pygame.display.update()
    ```

Adding sounds to the game

While the game is in progress, the sounds can be played using `pygame.mixer`. Refer to the following steps to find out how to do this:

1. Let's get started by importing `pygame.mixer`:

    ```
    import pygame.mixer
    ```

2. This is followed by initializing `pygame.mixer`:

    ```
    pygame.mixer.init()
    ```

3. The sounds that will be played when the game is launched or while the game is in progress have to be loaded:

```
menu_sound = pygame.mixer.Sound('8-bit-circus-music.wav')
moves_sound = pygame.mixer.Sound('ding.wav')
```

4. We chose to use sounds from *Free Sounds* (https://www.freesound.org). The sounds are available under Creative Commons License.

 Ding hits can be found at https://www.freesound.org/people/ adcbicycle/sounds/13952/ and *8 Bit Circus Music* can be found at https://www.freesound.org/people/bone666138/ sounds/198896/.

5. In the main menu, let's play the `8-bit-circus-music` file in an infinite loop (until the user launches a game or exits the menu).

```
menu_sound.play(-1)
```

6. The parameter `-1` indicates that the files need to be filed in a loop.

7. In order to stop playing the sound, the `stop()` method has to be called before launching the game:

```
menu_sound.stop() #stop playing the sound
runGame(isFirstGame)
```

8. The sound file is played in a loop once again after the game is over.

9. Similarly, the `ding` sound is played whenever the game AI (called the *computer* in the game) or the player has played a turn:

```
moves_sound.play() #Play ding sound
```

Objective complete – mission debriefing

We have completed the basic tweaks required for the game. In the next step, we will interface the arcade style buttons to the game.

Interfacing game inputs using the PiFace module

In this task, we will review interfacing the arcade style buttons (shown in the following image) to Raspberry Pi to play the game. In this task, we will just discuss the software part of the code.

Momentary arcade pushbutton switch (http://na.suzohapp.com/all_catalogs/pushbuttons/58-9111-L)

We will make use of the PiFace interface board available at `http://www.piface.org.uk/products/piface_digital/` to interface these buttons to Raspberry Pi. The board is a stackable add-on hardware that can be used to interface eight inputs and eight outputs. The PiFace comes with four tactile switches and we can get started with testing the inputs.

The main reason behind using the PiFace is that we need to monitor the switch states to determine there is a key press. The PiFace comes with an I/O expansion option and can be accessed through the SPI interface. These features enable simple control of the game inputs.

Prepare for lift off

1. Raspberry Pi's Serial Peripheral Interface (SPI) drivers need to enabled by editing the `/etc/modprobe.d/raspi-blacklist.conf` file using a text editor such as nano:

    ```
    sudo nano /etc/modprobe.d/raspi-blacklist.conf
    ```

    ❑   The drivers can be enabled by inserting an # before the following line:

    ```
    #blacklist spi-bcm2708
    ```

    ❑   The SPI drivers need to be loaded using the `modprobe` command:

    ```
    sudo modprobe spi-bcm2708
    ```

    ❑   The drivers/tools required to interface with the PiFace module can be installed as follows:

    ```
    wget http://pi.cs.man.ac.uk/download/old_install.txt
    ```

The installation packages for the PiFace module are available as Debian packages. Refer to the installation guide from `http://www.piface.org.uk/guides/`. If you install the Debian packages, the Python module imports and the methods used to read the inputs might also vary accordingly.

2. Let's rename the file and execute it:

```
mv install.txt install.sh
chmod +x install.sh
./install.sh
```

3. Once the required tools are installed, Raspberry Pi has to be restarted using the following command:

```
sudo reboot
```

4. Once Raspberry Pi has restarted, the emulator that comes along with the tool can be tested. The emulator enables you to test all inputs and outputs of the PiFace interface. The emulator can be launched from the command-line terminal as follows:

```
Piface/scripts/piface-emulator
```

5. The emulator interface would be something like the one shown in the following screenshot:

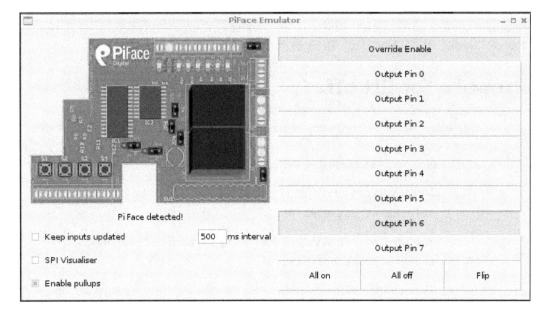

Engage thrusters

1. Let's test the buttons available on the PiFace module using a Python script:

```
import piface.pfio as pfio
```

2. The `piface.pfio` module needs to be imported and initialized:

```
pfio.init()
```

3. The `read_input()` method returns an 8-bit number that represents the input states of all the eight buttons:

```
while True:
  print(pfio.read_input())
```

4. Each bit of the 8-bit number corresponds to a digital input on the PiFace module. The following table shows the switch positions that are represented by bit positions:

S7	S6	S5	S4	S3	S2	S1	S0

Switch positions represented by bit positions

5. When a switch is pressed, a particular bit is set and this bit can be used to interpret the column position of the Connect Four game.

6. For example, when `S0` is pressed, the bit 0 is set and hence the 8-bit word value is 1. When `S1` is pressed, the bit 1 is set and the 8-bit word value is 2 and so on.

7. We ignore scenarios when two switches are pressed at the same time as the Connect Four game involves playing only one column at a time.

8. The Connect Four game was designed to be played using a mouse. Let's perform some tweaks to play it using buttons. Let's get started by commenting out the `getHumanMove()` function.

9. When the game is played using a mouse, the coin is actually dragged and dropped by the player. This needs to be simulated while using the buttons. In order to do so, let's create a copy of the `animateComputerMoving(board,column)` method and rename it as `animatePlayerMoving(board,column)`.

10. In the game, the computer plays the red colour coins while the human player plays with the black colour coins. So, let's change the `animatePlayerMoving(board, column)` method to simulate the human player's coin movements.

11. The following are the modifications required in the `animatePlayerMoving` method:

```
x = REDPILERECT.left
y = REDPILERECT.top
drawBoard(board, {'x':x, 'y':y, 'color':RED})
animateDroppingToken(board, column, RED)
```

12. Similarly, the main game loop also needs to be modified to simulate the human player's game moves:

```
if turn == HUMAN:

    animatePlayerMoving(mainBoard,0)
    makeMove(mainBoard, RED, 0)

    moves_sound.play()
if isWinner(mainBoard, RED):
    winnerImg = HUMANWINNERIMG
    break

turn = COMPUTER # switch to other player's turn
```

13. The next step is to interface the buttons to the game. The following code needs to be added under the human player's turn:

```
#wait for a button press
while column == 0:
    column = pfio.read_input()
    column_position = 0
if column == 1:
    column_position = 0
elif column == 2:
    column_position = 1
elif column == 4:
    column_position = 2
elif column == 8:
    column_position = 3
elif column == 16:
    column_position = 4
elif column == 32:
    column_position = 5
elif column == 64:
    column_position = 6
```

14. We use the `read_input()` function to detect any button press. When a button is pressed, the returned value can be anywhere between 1 and 64. The return value is used to identify the column position and the coin movement is simulated.

15. Similarly, the main menu of the game needs to be modified to be controlled using buttons. The game is launched when button 1 is pressed and the player leaves the game when a button is pressed:

```
if e.type == EVENT_CHANGE_STATE:
    if state == 0:
        rect_list,state = menu.update(e,state)
```

```
column = 0
while column == 0:
  column = pfio.read_input()
  pygame.display.update()
if column == 1:
  state = 1
elif column == 2:
  state = 2

if state == 1:
  menu_sound.stop()
  runGame(isFirstGame)
  isFirstGame = False
  state = 0
  prev_state = 1
elif state == 2 :
  print 'Exit'
  pygame.quit()
  sys.exit()
```

Objective complete – mini debriefing

In this task, we completed the transfer of controls to make use of the arcade style buttons. We will now proceed to the next stage where we will discuss the game AI, marquee design, and so on.

A brief description of the Connect Four Game AI

In this task, we will discuss the general mechanism of the game. We will discuss the function calls used, game flow, and a general idea of the game mechanism. It would be a good idea to follow this code review along with the game code available in this project.

Prepare for lift off

We are building this arcade game based on the code from *Making Games with Python & Pygame* by Al Sweigart (http://inventwithpython.com/makinggames.pdf). This book is an interesting read and it should enable us to build our own arcade game (not necessarily the Connect Four game).

Engage thrusters

1. Let's get started with reviewing the general structure of the game using the flowchart shown in the following diagram:

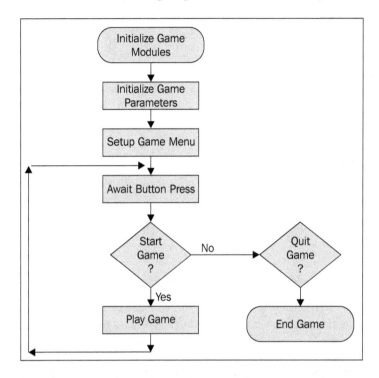

2. The first step is to import the modules required to launch and play the game. This includes the `pygame,` `pygame.mixer,` `piface,` and `serial` modules.

3. After importing the requisite modules, game parameters such as game difficulty, board size in terms of width and height, background color, window size, colors of the computer, and player coins are initialized.

4. The game menu is initialized and rendered on the game screen to await a button press by the player.

Main game loop

1. When the start button is pressed, the `runGame` function is called to start the game. If the game is being launched for the first time, the `isFirstGame` variable is set to `true`. The computer always plays first for the very first time after the game is launched and the first turn is randomized for consecutive plays.

2. When a new game is initialized, the `getNewBoard` method is called to create an empty board object to get started with the game. All game moves by the computer and the human player are recorded to this object. This is used to determine whether there is a winner as well as the computer to determine potential moves to play the game.

3. Once we enter the main game loop, the game loop is divided into two tasks, the computer and the human's turn.

4. When it is the player's turn, we wait for the player to play their turn using the buttons. When a button press is detected, using the `animatePlayerMoving` method, a coin drop is simulated. The game's board object is updated with the latest move.

5. This is followed by the computer's turn. The `getComputerMove` method calls the `getPotentialMoves` function to determine the best possible moves available for the computer's turn. Then, the computer's coin drop is simulated using the `animateComputerMoving()` method.

6. The game AI runs a check after each turn has been played to determine whether the player or the computer is a winner using the `isWinner` method.

7. If either of them has won the game, an image declaring the winner is chosen. The game also checks whether the game was a tie. When either of the earlier mentioned three events occur, the program breaks out of the game loop and displays the winner (or a tie) and waits for the start button event to return to the main menu. Consequently, this will enable you to start a new game.

Objective complete – mini debriefing

Now that the code review is complete, let's move on to the next task to implement a simple marquee and wire up the input buttons.

Marquee design and control (optional)

In this task, we will implement the marquee control for our arcade game. We will display information such as the player's turn (whether it is the computer or the human player's turn), the winner of the game at the end (or whether it was a tie), or game-specific messages on the marquee. We will use the Pi Lite LED Matrix display (`http://shop.ciseco.co.uk/pi-lite-lots-of-leds-for-the-raspberry-pi-1206-red/`) that can be used to scroll messages across the display.

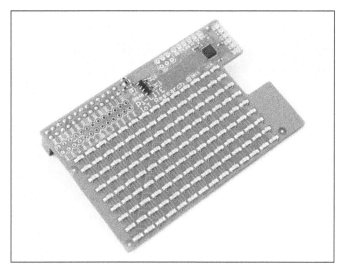

Pi Lite – Courtesy: The Ciseco PLC website

Prepare for lift off

The Pi Lite display can be purchased from the Ciseco PLC website (`http://shop.ciseco.co.uk/pi-lite-lots-of-leds-for-the-raspberry-pi-1206-red/`). The display costs about 33 USD.

One of the requirements is the **serial library**, which is required to control the display. It can be installed as follows:

```
sudo apt-get install python-serial
```

Once we are done installing the module, we should be able to import the module and start programming the messages in our game. The **Ciseco Pi-Lite** GitHub repository comes with examples such as the **Bar Scroll** example. It is essential that you download such examples and test if the python-serial module is functionally correct.

Engage thrusters

1. We will get started by importing the serial module and initializing the serial port parameters, including the baud rate and port name:

```
import serial
serialport = serial.Serial()
serialport.baudrate = 9600
serialport.timeout = 0
serialport.port = "/dev/ttyAMA0"
```

2. After initialization, the serial port is opened to start scrolling the messages across the display:

```
try:
  serialport.open()
 except serial.SerialException, e:
   sys.stderr.write("could not open port %r: %s\n" % (port, e))
```

3. As an example, we will display the **Welcome to Connect Four Game** message in the main game menu:

```
column = pfio.read_input()
serialport.write("Welcome to Connect Four Game")
pygame.display.update()
```

Objective complete – mini debriefing

In this task, we finished integrating the LED display to Raspberry Pi that runs the game.

Setup of the switches using a cardboard box

In this task, we will design our arcade game cabinet using cardboard. We will use cable ties to mount the components of our arcade game. We will leave it to the reader to design a better cabinet using tools of their choice.

Prepare for lift off

We should put together a monitor, Raspberry Pi, speakers, and the push buttons used to play the game. We also need plenty of cardboard to prototype the design of our cabinet.

Engage thrusters

1. Let's get started with mounting the switches. The switches will be mounted onto a cardboard box.

2. We get started by mounting the arcade style push buttons on a cardboard box. The arcade style push buttons used in this project require a hole that is 1.13 inches in diameter. Carefully create the holes using a sharp object.

[Do not hurt yourself while handling sharp objects. Parental supervision is required if children are working on this project.]

3. Once the mounting holes are cut out of the cardboard box, we need to mount the switches as shown in the following image. The switches are locked in place by a lock nut from the back side.

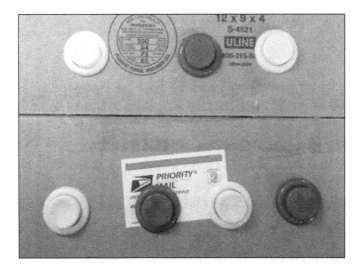

4. The next step is to interface the buttons to the PiFace module. The PiFace manual describes that the digital inputs have pull up resistors and hence the switches can be connected as shown in the figure that follows:

5. The common terminal of the button needs to be connected to the ground terminal of the PiFace module. The normally open (N.O.) terminal of the button is connected to the digital input terminals (S0 through S7) of the PiFace module.

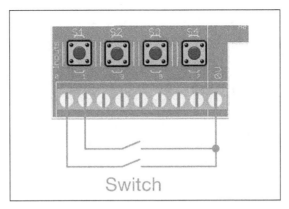

Suggested input connections provided by the PiFace manual

6. The next step is to connect a monitor to Raspberry Pi. The following figure shows a monitor with the Connect Four game launched and the switches mounted onto a cardboard box and interfaced with the PiFace module:

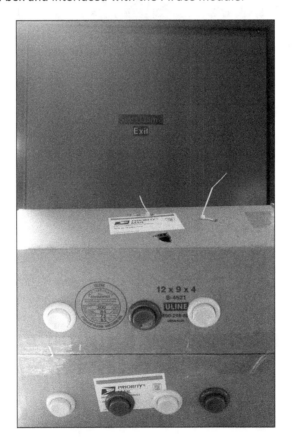

Objective complete – mini debriefing

In this task, we finished setting up the desktop Connect Four game using Raspberry Pi.

Mission accomplished

In this project, we accomplished the following:

1. We used a Python script for the Connect Four Game and tweaked it to our requirements.

2. We implemented input controls using arcade style switches.

3. We wrote a program to control the marquee.

4. We also set up things on a cardboard box to play the game.

Hotshot challenge

In this project, we performed control of the input switches as a blocking operation. Can you figure out how to monitor switch press events by starting multiple threads? How can we improve the speed of the game?

References

1. *Making Games with Python and Pygame* is available at `http://inventwithpython.com/makinggames.pdf`.

2. *PiFace Guides* can be found at `http://www.piface.org.uk/guides/`.

3. *Pi-Lite Users' Guide* can be found at `http://openmicros.org/index.php/articles/94-ciseco-product-documentation/raspberry-pi/280-b040-pi-lite-beginners-guide`.

Project 9

The Raspberry Pi-enabled Pet/Wildlife Monitor

In this project, we will discuss how the Raspberry Pi can interact with other devices on a network. This device can either be a laptop, an Arduino, or any other device connected to a network. We will make use of the capability of the Raspberry Pi to act as a control device in the network and implement a simple solution that can safely interact with our precious little animal friends.

Mission briefing

In this project, we will learn to build an interactive pet or wildlife (we call it wildlife in the context of animals that are not domesticated, for example, wild cats) monitor that can be monitored and controlled within a network (with some extra effort you should be able to control anywhere on the Web). This project presents three different possibilities where we can make use of the Raspberry Pi in combination with other devices to build an interactive device for pets that dispense treats to interface with devices that either interact with pets/feral cats/birds. This interactive device can either be a camera that captures a moment (for example, a wild bird coming and eating out of your bird feeder) or a relay board activated to feed treats to our animal friend while we are away from home.

This project has been presented as an example to help a person enhance the quality of life for their animal friends. This project should not be construed as a replacement of human interaction for our animal friends. We totally understand that pets ease the stress in our lives and this project presents some examples to make their lives better.

Why is it awesome?

We are demonstrating the capabilities of the Raspberry Pi while building a pet monitor. This can be adopted in any application where there needs to be exchange of information between devices. This project demonstrates the use of the Raspberry Pi in the betterment of our lives from another perspective. Our pets and other feral friends (for example, birds or feral cats) that visit us are our family members and we try our best to take care of them. Our goal in this project is to make the Raspberry Pi do our job better.

Your objectives

In this project, we will explore the following topics:

- Installing and testing the `python-twisted` framework
- Setting up and testing Spark Core to interact with appliances
- Installing and testing the Google Coder project on the Raspberry Pi
- A brief overview of a bird feeder that triggers a camera

Mission checklist

For this project, we will need:

1. A Raspberry Pi plus SD card (at least 4GB in size)
2. Any one of the following boards:
   - An Arduino Ethernet board (`http://arduino.cc/en/Main/arduinoBoardEthernet`)
   - A Spark Core board (`https://www.spark.io/`)
   - An Arduino Uno plus ESP8266 board (`http://www.banggood.com/ESP8266-Remote-Serial-Port-WIFI-Transceiver-Wireless-Module-p-947259.html`)
   - A few resistors and LEDs to test things out
   - A USB web camera or the Rapberry Pi's camera module

Installing and testing the python-twisted framework

In this task, we will review the `python-twisted` framework (`https://twistedmatrix.com/trac/`). The Twisted framework is an open source event-driven network engine that can be used to send control messages to other devices (for example, a pet feeder can be operated using Raspberry Pi to dispense solid food to our animal friends). The messaging protocol is called **AMP (Asynchronous Messaging Protocol)** which is available at `http://amp-protocol.net/`.

Prepare for lift off

The Raspberry Pi (with an SD card flashed with the OS image) connected to the Internet is needed for this task along with an Arduino Ethernet Board (or any one of the boards mentioned earlier in the checklist. Network connectivity is essential). We will install the `python-twisted` framework and review a quick example to exchange messages between Arduino and the Raspberry Pi.

Engage thrusters

1. The `python-twisted` framework can be installed from the terminal of the Raspberry Pi as follows:

   ```
   sudo apt-get install python-twisted
   ```

2. Once the installation is complete, it is time to review an example of the python-twisted framework to test the framework (`http://twistedmatrix.com/documents/current/_downloads/simpleserv.py`).

   1. In this task, we will launch a server on the Raspberry Pi and try to communicate to the server within the local network.

   2. Let's modify the preceding example to bind the `python-twisted` server to the IP address of Raspberry Pi so that we can exchange messages with other devices on the network. This device can either be an Arduino or a laptop.

   3. We will modify the `listenTCP` method to bind the server to the IP address of the Raspberry Pi and listen to incoming messages at the port address, `8000`.

      ```
      reactor.listenTCP(8000,factory,50,'192.168.1.89')
      ```

   4. The web server can be launched by executing a Python script.

   5. Now, using a laptop that is connected to the same network, let's modify the `simpleclient.py` script to send and receive messages to the server just launched on the Raspberry Pi (`https://twistedmatrix.com/documents/14.0.1/_downloads/simpleclient.py`).

6. In order to connect to the server launched on Raspberry Pi, the `connectTCP` method needs to be modified to include the IP address that the client has to connect:

```
reactor.connectTCP('192.168.1.89', 8000, f)
```

7. In this example, the Raspberry Pi is the server and the laptop is the client. The server in this example echoes all incoming messages. Thus, when the client connects and sends a message, the output will be something like:

```
Server said: Hello, World!
connection lost
Connection lost - goodbye!
```

3. Now that we have installed the server, let's discuss a simple Arduino sketch to interact with the server launched on the Raspberry Pi. The sketch is available along with this project's downloads (`TwistedFrameworkTest.ino`).

    1. We will get started by declaring an IP address object that includes the IP address of Raspberry Pi:

    ```
    //MAC Address of the Arduino
    byte mac[] = { 0x90, 0xA2, 0xDA, 0x0F, 0x02, 0xFC };
    //IP Address of the Raspberry Pi
    IPAddress server( 192, 168, 1, 89);
    ```

    2. The Arduino acts as a TCP client and connects to the Raspberry Pi:

    ```
    if (client.connect(server, 8000)) {
      Serial.println("connected");
      client.println("Hello, World!");
      client.println();
      //Lets wait for the client to read and
      //echo the message
      //Note: A second's delay is a bit excessive
      delay(1000);
      //If there is a response from the server
      //echo back the message
      Serial.println("Server says:");
      while(client.available()) {
        char c = client.read();
        Serial.print(c);
      }
      client.stop();
      Serial.println("Client Disconnected");
    } else {
      Serial.println("connection failed");
    }
    ```

3. The Arduino client connects to the Raspberry Pi and transmits the **Hello, World!** message. The Raspberry Pi echoes back the message to the Arduino client. A screenshot of the server's response to the client is shown as follows:

Interaction of the Arduino client with the Raspberry Pi

4. We demonstrated the ability to transmit and receive messages between Arduino and the Raspberry Pi.

Objective complete – mini debriefing

At the end of this project, we will discuss making use of the `python-twisted` framework and an Arduino Ethernet board to help you control a camera trigger or remotely dispense treats using a pet feeder.

Setting up and testing Spark Core to interact with appliances

In this task, we will set up Spark Core. It is a development board that makes bringing Wi-Fi to hardware very easy. We will use the Core for this project because we love the simplicity of the setup and operation. You can read more about Spark Core at the official website, `https://www.spark.io/`.

You are welcome to use a similar device of your choosing. A good alternative will be to use an Arduino with a Wi-Fi adapter/shield (for example, the ESP8266 Wi-Fi module can be found at `http://www.seeedstudio.com/wiki/WiFi_Serial_Transceiver_Module`) or if you prefer, an Ethernet shield (as discussed in the previous task of this project).

Prepare for lift off

In this task, we will set up the Spark Core. Power up the Spark Core using a micro-USB cable connected to a power source (5 V source). It can be powered using a battery pack, a laptop, or a 5 V USB wall wart. Based on your project needs, you can use a battery pack if the sensor node for the pet monitor has to be installed outdoors.

The easiest way to connect the Spark Core to your Wi-Fi network is through a phone application. This and other mechanisms are detailed on the Spark Core website (`http://docs.spark.io/connect/`). We will set up our Spark Core by downloading the application onto an Android phone and Samsung Galaxy S5 through the Google Play store (`https://play.google.com/store/apps/details?id=io.spark.core.android&hl=en`). The app searches for Spark Cores in range and if you supply the Wi-Fi password, it sends the code to the Core(s) and lets it connect to your Wi-Fi.

The SparkCore board

Engage Thrusters

We will warm up by implementing the LED example on Spark Core or something similar.

The documentation includes code to connect an LED with a resistor to the Core (`http://docs.spark.io/examples/`). We decided to do something even simpler. There is already an LED connected to pin D7 and we decided to turn this one on instead.

All the apps you need can be downloaded to a custom web page available for each Spark Core through a username and password.

Once you have set up the Core, you will create a username and password. For different Cores, you will need different usernames. Using this, you can go to the Spark home page (`http://www.spark.io/`) and click on the **Build** button. This takes you to the home page of the development environment.

Using this development environment, we created a simple LED blinking application:

```
void setup() {
  pinMode(7,OUTPUT);
}
void loop() {
// turn the LED on (HIGH is the voltage level)
  digitalWrite(7, HIGH);
// wait for a second
  delay(1000);
// turn the LED off by making the voltage LOW
  digitalWrite(7, LOW);
// wait for a second
  delay(1000);
}
```

 The preceding code is written in C programming language. If you are jumping directly to this project from other projects, we suggest that you familiarize yourself with the Arduino or Spark Core platform. Some learning resources are available at `https://learn.adafruit.com/search?q=Arduino`

As you can see, the app is quite simple; the app sets up the pin 7 as output. The program turns on the LED for a second and turns it off for one second.

Now, let's discuss an example that is more or less similar to the example discussed in the previous task:

```
TCPClient client;
// IP Address of the Raspberry Pi
byte server[] = { 192, 168, 1, 89 };
```

```
void setup()
{
  Serial.begin(9600);

  while(!Serial.available()) SPARK_WLAN_Loop();

  delay(1000);

  Serial.println("connecting...");

  if (client.connect(server, 8000)) {
    Serial.println("connected");
    client.println("Hello, World!");
    client.println();
    //Lets wait for the client to read and
    //echo the message
    //Note: A second's delay is a bit excessive
    delay(1000);
    //If there is a response from the server
    //echo back the message
      Serial.println("Server says:");
      while(client.available()) {
      char c = client.read();
      Serial.print(c);
    }
    client.stop();
    Serial.println("Client Disconnected");
  } else {
    Serial.println("connection failed");
  }
}

void loop()
{
//Nothing to do here
}
```

The only difference between the previous example and this example is that the latter uses the TCPClient class while the former uses the EthernetClient class.

Objective complete – mini debriefing

That's it. You now have Spark Core, all set up and ready to go, with your username, and your own page to download apps and collect and transmit data through the Core.

Installing and testing the Google Coder project on the Raspberry Pi

This is probably the simplest stage of the project as you should be familiar with setting up the Raspberry Pi for first use.

The Google Coder is a tool released by Google that enables people to learn web development using the Raspberry Pi. It is a tool that provides an intuitive learning process. After installing the Google Coder tool, we will test interfacing the GPIO pins of the Raspberry Pi to the web interface.

Prepare for lift off

We need to download the Google Coder image from its repository. The Google Coder image is available at `http://googlecreativelab.github.io/coder/`.

Engage thrusters

1. Let's get started with setting up Google Coder for the Raspberry Pi. Once the image is downloaded, we have to install the image onto an SD card. If you are not familiar with the installation of the Raspbian image onto an SD card, the first project of this book is really helpful (we think!).

2. Once the Raspberry Pi is powered up after flashing the SD card, MacBook users may launch the tool from a browser by going to `http://coder.local`.

3. Windows users have to install Apple's Bonjour Print Services for Windows (`http://support.apple.com/kb/DL999`). Once installed, the Google Coder tool can be launched using a Chrome browser. Now, the Google Coder platform can be accessed at `http://coder.local`.

4. The setup process is really simple. If everything went as planned, we should be able to see the landing page of the Google Coder application.

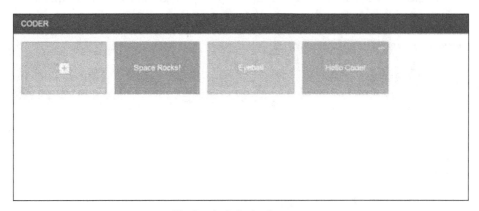

The Google Coder landing page

5. Let's test the *Blinky Lights* example from the Google Coder project available at `http://googlecreativelab.github.io/coder-projects/projects/blinky_lights/`. The example provides detailed instruction, including the circuitry and code required to set up a switch to read button states from the GPIO interface of the Raspberry Pi (We chose to skip the explanation as the example already provides a detailed elaboration of the example code).

6. The *Blinky Lights* example demonstrates the use of the `node.js` based GPIO helper (`https://www.npmjs.com/package/pi-gpio`) to read/write GPIO pins.

Objective complete – objective complete

We will make use of the three tasks discussed in this project to put together a trigger that comes to eat out of a bird feeder.

A brief overview of a bird feeder that triggers a camera

In this task, we will set up a bird feeder with a motion sensor. Whenever a bird flies into feed on the grains out of the feeder, the motion sensor is triggered to send a message to the Raspberry Pi. A camera module or a USB camera is connected to the Raspberry Pi, which captures some beautiful moments in our backyard.

Srihari Yamanoor (one of the authors of this book) has an extensive backyard where this bird feeder has been installed. Check out this book's website to find out whether we have captured any beautiful moments thus far!

Prepare for lift off

In order to build this interactive pet feeder, we need the following items:

- A pet feeder. (Available from home improvement stores, for example, Home Depot, Lowes, and so on).

- The PIR sensor (`http://www.adafruit.com/product/189`).

- Spark Core or any Wi-Fi enabled board.

- A USB battery pack (`http://www.adafruit.com/products/1959`).

- A small breadboard (`http://www.adafruit.com/products/64`).

- Raspberry Pi with a Twisted framework installed.

- A Raspberry Pi camera module with a lens attachment. For example, `http://store.cutedigi.com/raspberry-pi-camera-module-5mp-wide-angle-160-degree/`.

Engage thrusters

1. The first step involved in programming Spark Core is to detect the motion sensor events and publish those results to Raspberry Pi.

2. The sensor needs to be connected to SparkCore mounted on the breadboard as shown in the following figure:

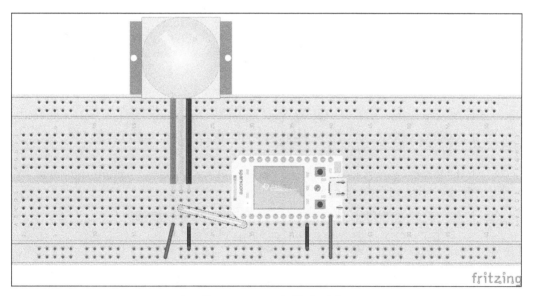

A motion sensor connected to Spark Core

3. We will modify the example from Adafruit that prints the motion sensor events (`https://learn.adafruit.com/pir-passive-infrared-proximity-motion-sensor/using-a-pir`).

4. Whenever a motion event is detected, we need to send an alert to the `python-twisted` server launched on Raspberry Pi:

```
if (client.connect(server, 8000)) {
  Serial.println("Motion Detected");
  client.println("Motion Detected");
  client.println();
  //Lets wait for the client to read and
  //echo the message
  //Note: A second's delay is a bit excessive
  delay(1000);

  client.stop();
  Serial.println("Client Disconnected");
} else {
  Serial.println("connection failed");
}
```

5. In order to take pictures of the bird feeder when there is an incoming motion detection event, the camera has to be interfaced to the Raspberry Pi as demonstrated in the video provided by the Raspberry Pi Foundation (`https://www.youtube.com/watch?v=GImeVqHQzsE`).

6. In order to trigger a camera to take a snapshot using the `python-twisted` server, we need the `picamera` module (`https://pypi.python.org/pypi/picamera`). It can be installed as follows:

```
sudo apt-get install python-picamera
```

7. Let's modify the `python-twisted` example, `simpleserv.py`, to import the `picamera` and `datetime` modules (to name the pictures captured by the camera using a timestamp).

8. If the incoming message is `Motion Detected`, we will take a picture and name the file using a timestamp.

9. In the callback method, `DataReceived`, let's capture an image:

```
with picamera.PiCamera() as camera:
  camera.start_preview()
  time.sleep(2)
  camera.capture('img{timestamp:%Y-%m-%d-%H-%M}.jpg')
```

A bird trigger

Objective complete – mini debriefing

Check out this book's website to look at th Raspberry Pi and Spark Sensor setup that is used to take pictures. This is really helpful to learn more about the birds in your neighborhood.

Alternatives and project ideas to consider

1. In this project, we discussed the examples using the Spark Core and the Arduino Ethernet board. Another example to consider is the EPS8266 module, which is available at `http://www.banggood.com/buy/Esp8266.html`, and costs about 3 USD. Refer to this book's website for setting up the ESP8266 module to emulate these examples.

2. In *Project 4*, *Christmas Light Sequencer*, we used a Power Switch Tail and a relay board example to control decorative appliances. Similarly, we can use them to control automatic pet feeders to dispense treats.

Mission accomplished

In this project, we interfaced built a small ecosystem of devices that were monitored by the Raspberry Pi. We used those examples to build a bird feeder!

Hotshot challenge

In this project, we discussed interfacing a sensor to take pictures of birds that come to feed from the bird feeder. Is it possible to upload the video feed to somewhere that's secure over the Internet? How do we do this?

Project 10

Raspberry Pi Personal Health Monitor

In this project, we will discuss implementing a solution where Raspberry Pi acts as a personal health monitor. We would like to dedicate this project to all the people who have been diagnosed with type 2 diabetes or any other lifestyle diseases. This project presents some tricks for those diagnosed with such lifestyle diseases.

 Please do not consider this project as an alternative to existing treatment and practices. This project's tricks will help you lead a better life. For example, your Raspberry Pi can remind you to take your prescribed medication (if any).

Mission briefing

In this project, we will build some solutions to address common problems encountered by people with lifestyle diseases. Similar to *Project 6, Raspberry Pi as a Personal Assistant*, this project presents different tips and tricks to lead a better life in each task. We will discuss examples where a person can build a simple web server to store his/her daily vital health parameters (for example, blood pressure, blood oxygen saturation levels (SpO2), and so on). Also, the server can help a person to remain physically active through the day, provide a quick recap of the e-mail parser, provide the event reminder tool from *Project 6, Raspberry Pi as a Personal Assistant* to remind a person about upcoming appointments, refill his/her prescriptions, and so on.

Why is it awesome?

We decided to write this project based on the personal experience of one of the authors' family member. It is quite stressful for a person when he/she is diagnosed with a chronic conditions such as type 2 diabetes. The person is subjected to stressful conditions related to change in daily food habits, developing a habit of consuming medication every day, and being mindful of what he/she eats every day whilst ensuring that their critical health parameters are intact. It is obviously difficult to accept a sudden change, and this project presents some options to mitigate such difficulties and bring the person's health back on track.

Your Hotshot objectives

In this project, we will review the following examples:

  ▸ Setting up a web server to record health parameters
  ▸ A simple physical exercise tool using Raspberry Pi
  ▸ Setting up an e-mail feed parser to refill a prescription as well as remind the user about an upcoming doctor's appointment
  ▸ A simple tool that reminds a person to take his/her pills

Mission checklist

It would be great to have the following components for this project:

  ▸ A Raspberry Pi along with an SD card (of at least 4GB in size) that has been flashed with an image and requisite power cable.
  ▸ An Arduino Ethernet board (`http://arduino.cc/en/Main/arduinoBoardEthernet`). This is completely optional.
  ▸ A tactile switch, resistors (10 K), and a piezoelectric buzzer (all these components are available from Radio Shack).
  ▸ It would be great to have two Raspberry Pi boards to build the physical exercise tool using Raspberry Pi.

Setting up a web server to record health parameters

In this task, we will build a simple web server that can be used to maintain critical health parameters. Let's consider a scenario where a person is diagnosed with high blood pressure. The doctor asks the patient to record his/her vital health parameters such as pulse, oxygen level, or blood pressure. For this situation, we will build a simple web page that records the data and stores it in a CSV file.

Prepare for lift off

We will be using the Flask framework (`http://Flask.pocoo.org/`) to deploy the web server on Raspberry Pi. We made use of the Flask framework in *Project 4, Christmas Light Sequencer*. Just in case you skipped through *Project 4, Christmas Light Sequencer*, a Python package manager such as `pip` or `easy_install` is required to install the Flask framework:

```
sudo apt-get install python-pip
```

After the installation of the Python package manager is complete, the Flask framework may be installed as follows:

```
sudo pip install Flask
```

Engage thrusters

1. We will modify this basic Flask framework example (`http://runnable.com/UhLMQLffO1YSAADK/handle-a-post-request-in-Flask-for-python`) to take input from a browser:

    ❑ In the frontend of the web server, let's create textboxes in the `form_submit.html` file where we can enter the blood pressure, oxygen saturation levels, and pulse data. The landing page will look like the one shown in the following figure (when opened in a browser):

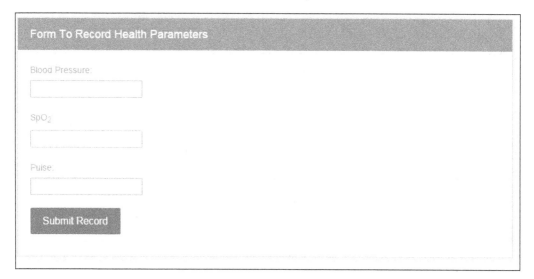

The form used to record vital health parameters

❏ In the Python script that launches the web server, we read the submitted parameters and write them to a CSV file along with a timestamp:

```
@app.route('/', methods=['POST'])
def record():
  #record all the data from the form
  bloodPressure=request.form['BloodPressure']
  SpO2=request.form['SpO2']
  pulse=request.form['pulse']
  #before writing to a csv file, log time stamps
  date = datetime.today().strftime('%Y-%m-%d')
  time = datetime.now().strftime('%H:%M:%S')
  logfile = open('static\\comments.csv', 'a')
  logfile.write(",".join([date,time,bloodPressure, SpO2,
pulse,'\n']))
    logfile.close()

    return render_template('form_action.
html',date=date,time=time,
    bloodPressure=bloodPressure, SpO2=SpO2,pulse=pulse
```

❏ Once we're done writing to the CSV file, we redirect the submitted form to a page that displays the recorded values along with the timestamp (as shown in the following figure):

Your Data Has Been Recorded To A CSV File!

Data Recorded: Blood Pressure: 120/80 Oxygen Saturation:99 Pulse:78

The page displayed after the results are recorded

2. It is possible to view the recorded data on the web page by reading the CSV file. We leave this for you to figure out (look at this book's website for the answer).

Objective complete – mini debriefing

We built a simple Flask-framework-based web server to record vital health parameters using Raspberry Pi. It is possible to e-mail the data at regular intervals using the `smtp` module in Python.

A simple exercise tool using the Raspberry Pi

In this task, we will review a fun example that enables a person to be physically active every 60 minutes.

Prepare for lift off

This example is based on the Twisted framework discussed in the previous project. It would be great to have two Raspberry Pi boards (set up with the SD card images and powered up) or an Arduino Ethernet board. A laptop that is connected to the same network as the Raspberry Pi is just as sufficient.

If you missed installing the Twisted framework in the previous project, the Twisted framework can be installed as follows:

```
sudo apt-get install python-twisted
```

 If the second device is a Raspberry Pi or a laptop that runs Linux, Mac, or Windows operating systems, the Twisted framework needs to be installed on the second device as well.

Engage thrusters

1. Let's perform a quick review of what we will build in this project:

   ❏ Let's consider two devices that can be connected to a network. One of the devices is a Raspberry Pi while the other device could either be an Arduino or a Raspberry Pi. We will review the code required to build this tool for both cases.

   ❏ These devices have to be installed at two extreme corners inside a house. This can be different floors of the house or the farthest corners of the house.

   ❏ A buzzer and a button will be connected to a Raspberry Pi.

   ❏ The buzzer would go off every 60 minutes on one of the devices. Someone has to walk up to the device and turn off the buzzer by pressing a button.

   This enables a person to get some physical activity by walking back and forth between the two devices (assuming the Raspberry Pi devices are installed far away from the person in the interest of gaining some physical activity).

This example is just a motivational tool and a casual reminder for the concerned person to remain physically active.

2. The buzzer and the switch are connected to the Raspberry Pi as shown in the following diagram:

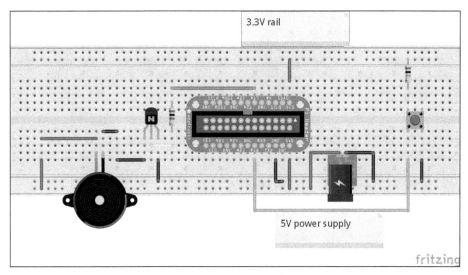

A button and buzzer schematic created using Fritzing

- ❏ The preceding breadboard representation shows an Adafruit Pi Cobbler mounted on a breadboard. Refer to *Project 4, Christmas Light Sequencer,* for a pictorial representation of how the Pi Cobbler needs to be connected to the Raspberry Pi.

- ❏ GPIO #25 of the Raspberry Pi is connected to the base of the NPN transistor, BC547. The transistor's collector pin is connected to the negative terminal of the buzzer. The other end of the buzzer is connected to 5 V. The emitter pin of the transistor is connected to the ground. The transistor acts as a switch and turns on the buzzer when the base pin is set to high.

- ❏ GPIO #18 of the Raspberry Pi is pulled up to 3.3 V and a tactile switch is connected to the GPIO switch. The other end of the switch is connected to the ground.

3. Let's perform a quick review of the twisted server code that runs on the Raspberry Pi. Similar to the previous project, this example is also a simple modification of the Twisted framework example, `simpleserver` (`http://twistedmatrix.com/documents/current/_downloads/simpleserv.py`).

❏ Let's create a class that takes care of setting off the buzzer when there is an incoming message:

```
#Declare inputs and outputs.
GPIO.setmode(GPIO.BCM)
GPIO.setup(18,GPIO.IN)
GPIO.setup(25,GPIO.OUT)
GPIO.setwarnings(False)

class AsyncTask:
  def __init__(self):
    self.run_state = True
  #avoiding the channel argument throws an error
  def terminate(self,channel):
    self.run_state = False

  def add_callback(self):
    GPIO.add_event_detect(18,GPIO.FALLING, callback=self.
terminate)

  def run(self):
    while self.run_state == True:
      GPIO.output(25,GPIO.HIGH)
      time.sleep(1)
      GPIO.output(25,GPIO.LOW)
      time.sleep(1)
    GPIO.remove_event_detect(18)
```

❏ In the `AsyncTask` class, the buzzer can be set off by triggering a separate thread to call the `run` function. This sets off the buzzer with a one-second interval.

❏ The `add_callback` method is used to turn off the buzzer when the button is pressed. The `add_event_detect` method waits for the state of GPIO #18 to change from high to low. This turns off the buzzer by setting `run_state` to `False`. While exiting the infinite loop, we remove the callback functions using the `remove_event_detect` method.

❏ When a client (Arduino, laptop, or another Raspberry Pi) sends a message to the server, the thread is initialized and a callback function is registered as follows:

```
async_task = AsyncTask()
async_task.add_callback()
thread = Thread(target=async_task.run, args=())
thread.start()
```

❑ To summarize, an incoming message triggers the buzzer and a person has to walk to the Raspberry Pi's location to turn off the buzzer.

4. If the client device that sends a message to the Raspberry Pi is a laptop that runs a Linux, Mac, or Windows operating system or the Raspberry Pi, it is sufficient to run the `simpleclient.py` example after modifying the code to change the server address to that of the Raspberry Pi (`https://twistedmatrix.com/documents/14.0.1/_downloads/simpleclient.py`).

5. In the preceding example, we demonstrate a single cycle to set off the buzzer. This can be repeated in cycles of 60 minutes using a batch script (in a Windows environment) or a shell script (Linux or Mac environment).

6. If the device is an Arduino, `EthernetClient` has to be initialized and connected to the Raspberry Pi to send a test message. This can be repeated in a 60-minute cycle:

```
Serial.println("connecting...");
  if (client.connect(server, 8000)) {
    Serial.println("connected");
    client.println("Hello, World!");
    client.println();
    //Lets wait for the client to read and
    //echo the message
    //Note: A second's delay is a bit excessive
    delay(1000);
    //If there is a response from the server
    //echo back the message
     Serial.println("Server says:");
     while(client.available()) {
       char c = client.read();
       Serial.print(c);
     }
    client.stop();
    Serial.println("Client Disconnected");
  } else {
    Serial.println("connection failed");
  }
```

A mini project idea

It will be fun to install a number of Raspberry Pi boards in the same network and implement an asynchronous messaging protocol. This protocol can set off buzzers as a chain reaction to encourage more physical activity. Please note that this may annoy other members of the household.

Objective complete – mini debriefing

We discussed a tool that can annoy a person to remain physically active.

Setting up an e-mail feed parser to refill a prescription as well as remind the user about an upcoming doctor's appointment

In this task, we will discuss setting up an LED to alert a person about an incoming e-mail to refill a prescription or when there is an upcoming doctor's appointment.

Just in case you skipped through *Project 6, Raspberry Pi as a Personal Assistant*, the `python-feedparser` tool and the `python-gdata` tool have to be installed:

```
sudo apt-get install python-feedparser
sudo apt-get install python-gdata
```

 This task is similar to the e-mail notifier we set up in *Project 5, Internet of Things Example – An E-mail Alert Water Fountain*. We will just discuss a minor modification to blink an LED when there is an e-mail in the inbox to refill a prescription.

Engage thrusters

1. We will get started by checking for any new incoming e-mails:

   ```
   email = feedparser.parse(proto+username+":"+password+"@"+server+pa
   th)
   ```

2. Let's assume the prescription refill reminder e-mail subject is called *Walgreens*. We will iteratively check through each entry and trigger an LED alert:

   ```
   for mail in email.entries:
     if mail.title == "Walgreens":
       async_task = AsyncTask()
       async_task.add_callback()
       thread = Thread(target=async_task.run, args=())
       thread.start()
   ```

   - An asynchronous task can be triggered to blink an LED until the alert is acknowledged by pressing a button. The circuitry is similar to the one discussed in the previous task.

3.   This enables a person to respond to an e-mail and refill his/her prescription when necessary. This prevents a refill reminder getting buried among e-mails and enables the person to keep a tab on prescription delays.

Setting up a reminder for doctor's appointments

This is also similar to the event notifier that we discussed in *Project 6, Raspberry Pi as a Personal Assistant*. Let's assume that all doctor's appointments are saved in the calendar as `Doctor's appointment`. It is possible to prominently display all upcoming doctor's appointments as follows:

```
for i, an_event in enumerate(feed.entry):
  if an_event.title.text == "Doctor's appointment":
    print '\t%s. %s' % (i, an_event.title.text,)
```

In the preceding example, we are just printing it to a console. You can perhaps make use of a display, for example, an OLED display that is controlled via a serial port, and display it at a prominent location.

Objective complete – mini debriefing

In this task, we completed the setup of an e-mail notifier to refill prescriptions and a reminder for an upcoming doctor's appointment.

A simple tool that reminds a person to take his/her pills

In this task, we will build a simple tool that reminds a person to take his/her pills on time. The circuitry required for this example is similar to the examples discussed in the previous tasks. We are discussing this example because it is difficult for someone to develop a habit of taking their medication on time. It is critical that people identified with chronic conditions do not miss their prescription schedule.

Prepare for lift off

We extensively discussed interfacing the buzzer to a Raspberry Pi in the previous task. It'll be nice to have an enclosure for the pillbox reminder. An example of a pill reminder is available from **instructables** at `http://www.instructables.com/id/The-Pill-Reminder/`. We will only discuss how to trigger the buzzer at a selected time of the day.

Engage thrusters

Let's say a person has to take his/her prescribed pills at 9:30 in the morning; a buzzer can be triggered using the `datetime` module in Python:

```
while True:
  t = datetime.datetime.now()
  if t.hour == 9 and t.minute == 30:
    async_task = AsyncTask()
    async_task.add_callback()
    thread = Thread(target=async_task.run, args=())
    thread.start()
    break
```

Other project ideas

Similar to the examples discussed earlier, it is also possible to set reminders to sync pedometer data, go to the gym, or even record the health parameters discussed earlier in this project.

Objective complete – mini debriefing

In this task, we completed the pillbox reminder set up to help us take our medication on time.

Mission accomplished

In this project, we discussed several examples of Raspberry Pi acting as a personal health monitor using a simple concept. This can be adapted for different scenarios according to your creativity.

Hotshot challenge

How can we use Raspberry Pi to enhance the lives of senior citizens?

Project 11

Home Automation using Raspberry Pi

In this project, we will review some automation examples using Raspberry Pi. These examples can be considered as projects that can be executed over a weekend.

Mission briefing

In this project, we will discuss different options available for automation at home using Raspberry Pi. The examples use a similar concept (more or less) and you can pick the tasks of your choice and turn your home into a smart home.

Why is it awesome?

A quick web search yields a lot of projects related to home automation using Raspberry Pi. We have tried to keep this project unique by ensuring that it is simple enough to be executed over a weekend (though some examples might appear repetitive if you have been reading through the projects in their correct order), while incorporating feedback from projects available all over the Web.

Your objectives

We will discuss the following examples in this project:

▶ A simple example that controls limited indoor and outdoor lighting in the evening

▶ A customary web server example

▶ Turning on a lawn sprinkler only when there is a no rain forecast!

Mission checklist

The following hardware items are required for this project:

1. Raspberry Pi along with the necessary accessories (an SD card—at least 4GB in size, 1A USB power supply, and a micro-USB power cable).

2. Power Switch Tail II from Adafruit that is available at `http://www.adafruit.com/product/268`.

3. Ethernet cables/Wi-Fi adapter (optional, needed to connect the Raspberry Pi to a network).

4. Sensors of your choice. For example, Soil moisture sensor.

5. General hardware from the local store (this depends upon the reader's project requirements).

6. Arduino Ethernet Board (optional) available at `http://arduino.cc/en/Main/arduinoBoardEthernet`.

We will install the software prerequisites as we review each example in this project.

A simple example that controls limited indoor and outdoor lighting in the evening

Let's consider a scenario where a person lives in a neighborhood that is not so well lit. In winter, the temperatures are usually extreme in cities such as Chicago and the sun usually sets around 5 p.m. The poorly lit neighborhood along with the cold weather makes it difficult for a person to enter their home.

We will build a simple solution that turns on a light (that can be either an outdoor or indoor hallway light) that speeds up the process of entering a building.

Prepare for lift off

In this example, we will make use of PowerSwitch Tail 2 (sold by Adafruit Industries: `http://www.adafruit.com/product/268`) to turn on/off the lights.

The Powerswitch tail is rated to control appliances rated to operate at 110V and it can switch resistive loads up to 15A. The PowerSwitch Tail 2 can switch on/off appliances when it is activated by a 3-12V DC signal.

One main advantage of using the PowerSwitch Tail 2 is that it is opto-isolated (opto-isolation ensures that Raspberry Pi is protected from any transient voltages while turning on/off the lights) and provides a safe alternative to interfacing electrical appliances to Raspberry Pi. The image below shows a PowerSwitch Tail 2 available from `http://www.adafruit.com`.

Power tail switch II – Photo courtesy: adafruit.com

Software prerequisites

We will need the repository tool Git. This can be installed as follows:

```
sudo apt-get git-core
```

Engage thrusters

1. PowerSwitch Tail 2's datasheet (`http://www.adafruit.com/datasheets/PST%20II%20product%20insert.pdf`) provides a schematic description of the internal circuitry of PowerSwitch Tail 2.

    ❑ PowerSwitch Tail 2 is connected to Raspberry Pi as shown in the following figure. The **in+** terminal of the switch is connected to the GPIO #17 of Raspberry Pi, while the **in-** terminal is connected to the ground pin of Raspberry Pi.

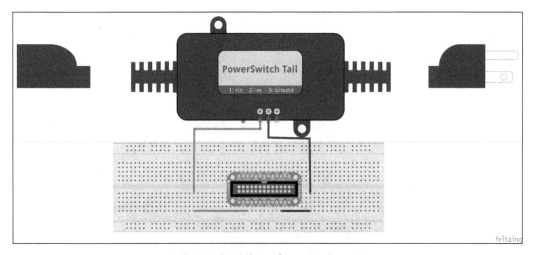

PowerSwitch Tail 2's interface to Raspberry Pi

    ❑ The power cord to the lighting equipment needs to be connected to PowerSwitch Tail 2.

 It is assumed that you are familiar with some minor rewiring to connect indoor/outdoor lighting appliances. Prior training is required to handle such electrical hardware. If you are not familiar with handling rewiring, it is best to connect an off-the-shelf electrical appliance.

2. Let's review the code for an example where the lights need to be turned on between 5:30 p.m. and 10:45 p.m. everyday.

    ❑ We get started by creating Unix timestamps for the start and end times (Unix timestamps refers to the time elapsed since January 1, 1970 in seconds. More information is available at `http://en.wikipedia.org/wiki/Unix_time`):

```
#Get current time
  now = datetime.datetime.now()
```

```
#Create datetime objects
   startTime = datetime.datetime(now.year,now.month,now.
day,17,30,0)
   endTime = datetime.datetime(now.year, now.month,now.
day,22,45,0)

   #Create unix time stamps
   unixStart = (startTime - datetime.datetime(1970,1,1)).
total_seconds()
   unixEnd = (endTime - datetime.datetime(1970,1,1)).total_
seconds()
   unixNow = (now - datetime.datetime(1970,1,1)).total_
seconds()
```

❑ The Unix timestamps are used to check whether it is time to turn on/off the appliances:

```
if ( unixStart <= unixNow <= unixEnd):
   GPIO.output(25,GPIO.HIGH)
   while ( unixStart <= unixNow <= unixEnd):
      now = datetime.datetime.now()
      unixNow = (now - datetime.datetime(1970,1,1,0,0,0)).
total_seconds()
      print "Triggered", now.hour,":",now.minute,":",now.
second
      sleep(1)
      GPIO.output(25,GPIO.LOW)
```

Objective complete – mini debriefing

Yay! We are done with a simple automation task of keeping the lights on at a given time period everyday.

Alternative solutions and some project ideas to consider

1. If it is not possible to install Raspberry Pi right next to the power tail switch, it is possible to interface the PowerSwitch Tail 2 to an Arduino Ethernet board and controlled by Raspberry Pi using the Twisted framework example (hint: refer to the examples from the previous project, *Project 10, Raspberry Pi Personal Health Monitor*). This enables you to control a network of devices using Raspberry Pi.

2. One alternative to consider if it is not possible to purchase a PowerSwitch Tail 2—SparkFun has an excellent tutorial on building a controllable AC power outlet (https://www.sparkfun.com/tutorials/119).

3. In this example, we assumed that the lights will be turned on between the selected time slots. It is also possible to turn on the lights by determining the sunset time. NOAA provides information on calculating sunset times, which is available at `http://www.esrl.noaa.gov/gmd/grad/solcalc/calcdetails.html`.

4. Another alternative to turning/off lighting appliances—it would be a great idea to make coffee everyday using PowerSwitch Tail 2. If the coffee maker is filled with water and the coffee pods/filter are replaced, the coffee maker will be turned on at the chosen time! We will have our coffee ready right after getting out of bed.

> PowerSwitch Tail 2 is designed for resistive loads and especially for limited use. Do not try to use it with heavy inductive loads such as a motor. This tool is strictly recommended for those who are knowledgeable with the fundamentals of electrical engineering.

A customary web server example

Any home automation project using Raspberry Pi yields a lot of examples that involves building a web server that controls appliances within a local network that takes care of securing the place using electromechanical locks. We will build a simple web server that can be used to turn off an LED from a web page. This concept can be expanded to control multiple appliances and read sensor data from the GPIO interface of Raspberry Pi.

> This task is meant for absolute beginners who are not familiar with Python web framework tools. We are discussing this example considering some readers might jump right to *Project 11, Home Automation Using Raspberry Pi*.

Prepare for lift off

We will be building a web server using a Flask framework (`http://flask.pocoo.org/`). The Flask framework can be installed as follows:

```
sudo apt-get install python-pip
sudo pip install Flask
```

Engage thrusters

1. The first part is setting up the landing page. When a user enters the address of the web server, the web page would be something like what is shown in the following screenshot. The HTML page consists of a single button called **Sample Button**.

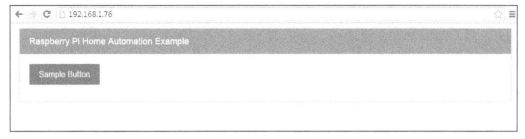

A flask framework-based web server

2. When a button is clicked, the incoming POST request is used to switch the states of the LED from ON to OFF and vice versa:

```
@app.route('/', methods=['POST'])
def record():
  #record all the data from the form
  global state
  if state == False:
    state = True
  else:
    state = False
  GPIO.output(25,state)
  return render_template('form_submit.html')
```

3. The web server can be launched from the IP address of Raspberry Pi. The web page should be accessible from `http://192.168.1.76:75`:

```
# Run the app :)
if __name__ == '__main__':
  app.run(
    host="0.0.0.0",
    port=int("75")
  )\
```

The web server example is available along with this project. Check this book's website for more examples.

Objective complete – mini debriefing

Using the simple concept explained earlier, it is possible to control any appliance (by interfacing some control device such as the power switch tail to Raspberry Pi's GPIO pins). It is also possible to read sensor states as well as track any special information. For example, it is possible to track the status of a package that is expected to be delivered. USPS provides status of shipments that can be displayed on the web page (for more information on APIs, check out `https://www.usps.com/business/web-tools-apis/welcome.htm`).

In all these examples, we reviewed control appliances using Raspberry Pi within a local network. In the later task of this project, we will review controlling the device from anywhere over the Internet.

Turning on a lawn sprinkler only when there is no rain forecast!

This example was inspired by a comment on an article related to Home Automation using Raspberry Pi. The commenter mentioned:

> *The only home automation that I'm interested in (and still haven't seen) is something that'll turn off my lawn sprinklers if it's rained a certain amount in the preceding days or if it's raining on the day that the sprinklers are programmed to go on.*

We decided to whip up a quick example that would turn on the sprinkler when it is not going to rain on a particular day.

Prepare for lift off

In order to check the weather forecast, we need to make the `python-weather-api` library (the library is distributed with MIT license). We will make use of the NOAA API. The library can be downloaded using the `wget` command:

```
wget https://launchpad.net/python-weather-api/trunk/0.3.8/+download/
pywapi-0.3.8.tar.gz
```

The source files are available in a compressed folder. The contents of the compressed file can be extracted as follows:

```
tar -xvzf pywapi-0.3.8.tar.gz
```

Once extracted, the library can be installed as follows:

```
python setup.py build
sudo python setup.py install
```

We also need a flow control valve similar to this one sold on **SparkFun** available at
`https://www.sparkfun.com/products/10456`.

Engage thrusters

1. NOAA (`http://www.weather.gov/`) provides weather data generated from the
   weather stations situated in different cities. Each city's weather station has a unique
   four-letter code. For example, Chicago, Illinois' code is KORD. We will make use of
   this four-letter code to retrieve the weather forecast for a city.

2. The weather data is retrieved using the `pywapi` library as follows:

```
def main():
    pp = pprint.PrettyPrinter(indent=4)

    while True:
        result = pywapi.get_weather_from_noaa('KORD')
        pp.pprint(result['weather'])
        sleep(10)
```

3. We will turn on the sprinkler only if the weather forecast (available under the
   weather keyword) is anything other than Rain, Light Rain, or Thunderstorm:

```
if (result['weather'] != 'Light Rain' or
    result['weather'] != 'Rain' or
    result['weather'] != 'Thunderstorm'):
        GPIO.output(25,GPIO.HIGH)
```

4. The sprinkler can be turned on using a transistor switching circuit and a relay.
   (If you are not familiar with transistor switching circuit and relays, *Project 4,
   Christmas Light Sequencer* provides information about a transistor switching
   circuit in extensive detail).

5. It has not been demonstrated here but the `pywapi` module needs to be used in
   conjunction with the `datetime` module to turn on the sprinkler at selected times
   of day.

Objective complete – mini debriefing

If it is not possible to interface the solenoid valve directly to Raspberry Pi, as the solenoid
valve can only be interfaced to an Arduino and controlled using the `python-twisted`
framework.

In states such as California where there are sometimes severe droughts, it is common
practice to save water from drain pipes using barrels. The `pywapi` module can be used to
replace the barrels if there is an upcoming rain forecast.

Gaining remote access to your Raspberry Pi to control appliances

It is possible to remotely log in to Raspberry Pi using **SSH** (**Secure Shell**). An organization called Weaved (`http://www.weaved.com/`) provides the capabilities to log in.

The tutorial available from `https://www.juicypi.io/access-your-raspberry-pi-anywhere-in-the-world-using-weaved/` provides detailed instructions to install the requisite tools.

This enables you to control the devices interfaced to Raspberry Pi.

Some project ideas to consider

▶   In houses with long hallways, it is not always possible to hear the doorbell ring from the far end of the house. It is possible to place a force sensitive resistor (`https://www.sparkfun.com/products/9375`) to track any visitors to the house. Likewise, it is possible to track packages left on the doormat.

▶   In *Project 6, Raspberry Pi as a Personal Assistant* (the personal assistant project), we built a small enclosure to keep track of keys using a reed switch. A similar concept can be used to track items using a reed switch.

▶   There is a wireless protocol called Z-Wave that was specifically designed for home automation purposes. Raspberry Pi can be turned into a control centre to wirelessly control appliances using the Z-Wave modules. Raspberry compatible modules are available for sale at `http://razberry.z-wave.me/` (check out this book's site for some examples).

▶   In *Project 5, Internet of Things Example – An E-mail Alert Water Fountain*, we built a web server that can set colors of the RGB LED strip. There are some interesting ideas to decorate our homes with these RGB LED strips (`http://www.usledsupply.com/shop/install/project-photos-and-ideas.html`).

▶   GE Appliances has come up with an interesting development tool that can be used to control products from GE. This tool in combination with Raspberry Pi (running Twisted server) can be used to control GE products in someone's home. In the future, all GE appliances will be capable of being connected to a smart devices network.

Mission accomplished

In this project, we looked into different solutions that can be implemented using Raspberry Pi over a weekend. We reviewed some basic examples that can be possibly tweaked to turn a home into a smart one.

Project 12

Using a Raspberry Pi for Science and Education

In this project, we will review some examples of how the Raspberry Pi can be used to educate ourselves. We will review examples of how to use the Raspberry Pi for self-improvement or educating children in the field of science.

Mission briefing

In this project, we will review some examples to demonstrate how the Raspberry Pi can be used to educate ourselves for self-improvement or demonstrate a simple physics experiment.

Why is it awesome?

The Pi, as you have seen in the last few projects, offers you immense functionality, and was basically designed to encourage learning computer science at an affordable cost. As we have seen, the possibilities of building gadgets using the Raspberry Pi are endless, making this an awesome segue into self-improvement and science.

Your Hotshot objectives

In this project, we will discuss the following examples:

- ▶ Improving your vocabulary using the Raspberry Pi
- ▶ Raspberry Pi and Khan Academy
- ▶ Building a science fair exhibit using the Raspberry Pi

Improving your vocabulary using the Raspberry Pi

As an example of self-improvement using the Raspberry Pi, we will implement an example that retrieves the word of the day using the Wordnik API (`https://www.wordnik.com/`).

Prepare for lift off

We need to install the Wordnik Python client (distributed under the Apache License) available as a Python package:

```
sudo pip install wordnik
```

The next step is to obtain an API key to make use of the API. This can be obtained by registering for an account with Wordnik and requesting an API key (`http://developer.wordnik.com/`).

Once the installation is complete, it is time to review the example.

 The Wordnik API is merely being demonstrated as an example. Refer to the API terms of agreement to determine how the API can be used in a commercial application.

Engage thrusters

1. Let's review an example that fetches the word of the day using the Wordnik API. The first step is to import the Wordnik Python client:

   ```
   from wordnik import *
   ```

2. The next step is to create a client that initializes the API to access the word list:

   ```
   url='http://api.wordnik.com/v4'
   key='API Key'
   client=swagger.ApiClient(key,url)
   ```

3. The next step is to initialize the Wordnik API and retrieve the word of the day:

```
words = WordsApi.WordsApi(client)
example = words.getWordOfTheDay()
```

4. The returned object is a `WordOfTheDay` object (`https://github.com/wordnik/wordnik-python/blob/master/wordnik/models/WordOfTheDay.py`). Let's print the word, definition, and the published date:

```
string = 'The Word of the Day is ' + example.word +'.'
print string
string = 'Definition: '+example.definitions[0].text
print string
string = 'Date = '+example.publishDate.strftime("%D")
print string
```

5. The output of this Python script is something like the one shown here:

```
The Word of the Day is asportation.
Definition: The felonious removal of goods from the place where
they were deposited.
Date = 01/19/15
```

6. Now, this word of the day can be displayed on a screen at some prominent location using a GUI tool such as Tkinter (`http://zetcode.com/gui/tkinter/`) and updated every 24 hours. Refer to this book's website for some ideas.

Objective complete – mini debriefing

In this task, we reviewed an example of how to use your Raspberry Pi for self-improvement; similarly, there are APIs from other sources that provide a quote of the day, joke of the day, and so on.

Raspberry Pi and Khan Academy

In this task, we will review an example that enables working on math exercises from Khan Academy (`https://www.khanacademy.org/`). Khan Academy is a non-profit educational organization that provides free learning resources for various subjects, including math and computer science. In this example, we will host a simple web server on a Raspberry Pi that hosts the exercises from Khan Academy locally. This enables customization of the learning tools to the user's needs. For example, it can be hosted on a network that is not connected to the Internet and we can customize content from Khan Academy to help someone improve on their math skills.

The first step is to clone the repository on a Raspberry Pi:

```
git clone https://github.com/Khan/khan-exercises
```

Once the repository is cloned, it is time to launch the web server!

> The exercises are distributed under a non-commercial license while the web server framework is distributed under an MIT license. You must be aware of the license agreements when trying to make use of resources from Khan Academy.

The launch of the server involves a single step. After switching to the `khan-exercises` directory, the web server can be launched as follows:

```
python -m SimpleHTTPServer
```

The web server can be accessed on a local network by using your Raspberry Pi's IP address from a browser using `http://192.168.1.98:8000/khan-exercises/exercises/`.

The following is a screenshot of the web server hosted on a Raspberry Pi:

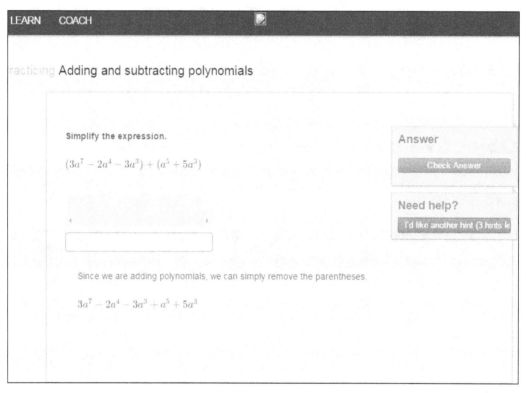

Khan Academy exercises on a local server

Some ideas to consider

We use this web server to solve puzzles using the Raspberry Pi. It can be useful to sharpen your mental acuity while killing time.

Building a science fair exhibit using the Raspberry Pi

In this task, we will build a simple physics experiment controlled by the Raspberry Pi. This can be used to explain how things such as a solar panel, windmill, and so on work. In this example, we will build a windmill experiment that can possibly be used as a demonstrative exhibit at a science fair.

Prepare for lift off

We need a windmill generator kit from a hobby store (for example, `http://amzn.com/ B0016PBH9Q`). The kit needs to be put together leaving the leads of the DC motor exposed.

Engage thrusters

1. The DC motor of the wind energy kit needs to be interfaced to the Raspberry Pi GPIO pin as shown in the following Fritzing schematic:

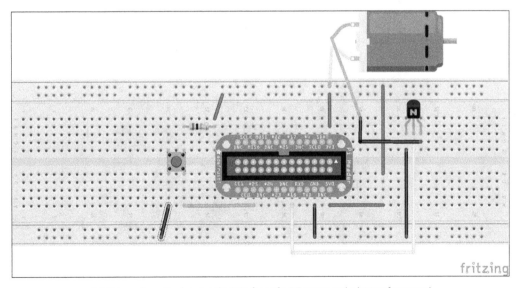

A Fritzing schematic showing the interface of a DC motor and a button for control

2. Since the DC motor is interfaced to your Raspberry Pi's GPIO #18, it can be turned on (we are making use of the `RPi.GPIO` libraries; refer to previous projects if you are not familiar with `RPi.GPIO`):

```
import RPi.GPIO as GPIO
GPIO.setmode(GPIO.BCM)
GPIO.setup(18,GPIO.OUT)

GPIO.output(25,GPIO.HIGH)
```

3. When a visitor at the exhibition would like to know how a windmill works, an instructional audio recording (the download available with this project merely plays a test MP3 file) can be played at the press of a button as follows:

```
def my_callback(channel):
  os.system('mpg321 recording.mp3 &')

GPIO.add_event_detect(25, GPIO.FALLING,callback=my_callback)
```

4. The following image shows a windmill generator kit interfaced to a Raspberry Pi:

A windmill generator kit

Objective complete – mini debriefing

Your Raspberry Pi can also be used to build something that tests the skills of people at a science fair or to provide entertainment (raffle draw, puzzle, and so on).

Some simple educational experiments using the Raspberry Pi

1. A software tool that alerts when the international space station flies by your vicinity can be found at `http://issabove.com/iss-above-and-the-raspberry-pi/`.

2. A collection of scientific experiment articles using the Raspberry Pi can be found at `http://www.raspberrypi.org/the-raspberry-pi-in-scientific-research/`.

3. Scratch is a graphical programming tool developed by MIT to motivate children to get started with learning to program. Scratch can be found at `http://www.raspberrypi.org/tag/scratch/`.

Hotshot challenge

Is it possible to build a receptionist robot like the one shown at the following link using the Raspberry Pi? Refer to `http://roboceptionist.org/project.htm` for more information.

Project 13
Tips and Tricks

In this project, we will discuss tips and tricks to overcome any problems one might encounter with Raspberry Pi. We also provide project ideas, general information, and a dissection of the Raspberry Pi itself.

Mission briefing

In this book, we discussed different projects, spanning different difficulty levels. Before wrapping up this book, we would like to share our experience about the challenges we encountered and share some tips and resources to overcome situations that you might encounter and possible solutions for them. We will also discuss possible project ideas that you can try to implement over a weekend. We will go into each aspect briefly.

Why is it awesome?

This project shares tips and tricks, provides project ideas, and discusses solutions to problems generally encountered in DIY projects.

Your objectives

In this project, we will discuss the following:

▸ Setting up Raspberry Pi as a development platform

▸ Project ideas that can be implemented over a weekend

▸ Remotely logging in to Raspberry Pi from anywhere on the Internet

▸ Problems that might be encountered while using Raspberry Pi

▸ Cool add-on hardware sources developed for the Raspberry Pi platform

▸ Useful resources for Raspberry Pi

Mission checklist

Have your curiosity, attention and passion at the ready.

Setting up Raspberry Pi as a development platform

Raspberry Pi is currently the most basic, ideal hardware environment to get started with learning to code in a particular language or advanced systems development.

#1 – Simple trick for Python development via remote login

While writing this book, we found it convenient to write Python scripts on our laptop/desktop, copy them over to Raspberry Pi, and test them via remote login. This was especially useful when we had Raspberry Pi controlling interfaced to tools on a Christmas tree. It is difficult to set up a monitor and keyboard for Raspberry Pi and work from there.

We used WinSCP (http://winscp.net/eng/index.php—since we were using a laptop running Windows) to transfer files from the laptop to Raspberry Pi. Then, we used the PuTTY SSH client (http://www.putty.org/) for a remote login to Raspberry Pi and tested the scripts:

> ▶ In order to remotely log in to Raspberry Pi or transfer files using WinSCP, OpenSSH is required. The Raspbian Wheezy image comes with SSH installed and enabled by default.

> ▶ Let's log in after downloading and installing WinSCP. The username would be pi and the password raspberry (unless you've changed the default password).

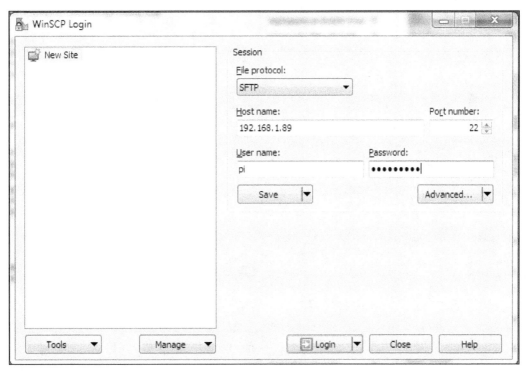

The WinSCP login window

▶ The next step is it to locate the files to be transferred on the local machine as well as identifying the folder where the files need to be copied to Raspberry Pi. The files on the local machine are located on the left-hand side, while the files on Raspberry Pi are located on the right-hand side of the window.

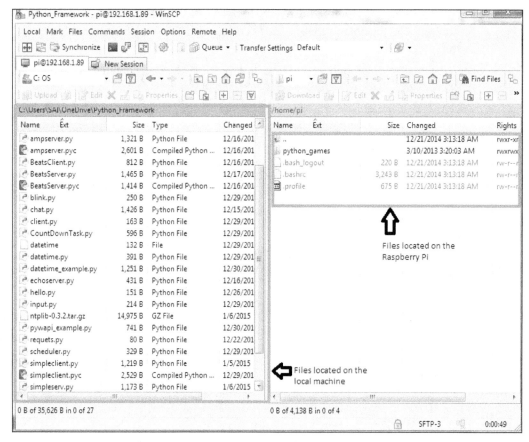

Transferring files using WinSCP

▸ Once the files are transferred, we can make use of PuTTY for remote login to Raspberry Pi. As shown in the following figure, we can connect to the Raspberry Pi using the IP address of Raspberry Pi and log in using the credentials provided earlier.

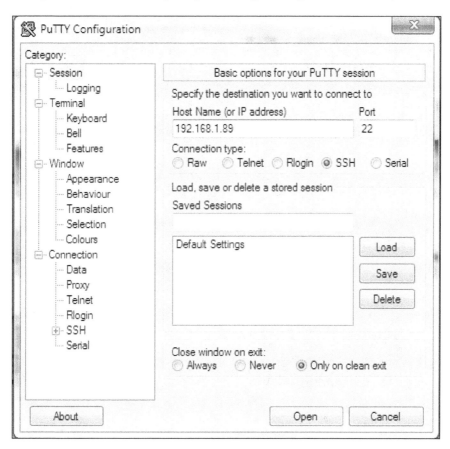

Connecting to Raspberry Pi using PuTTY

#2 Web development using Google Coder

Google released an open source tool based on the Raspberry Pi platform called Coder (`http://googlecreativelab.github.io/coder/`). We made use of the Google Coder tool in *Project 9, The Raspberry Pi-enabled Pet/Wildlife Monitor*. Google Coder is an open source tool to learn web development, but its use has expanded and as an open source tool, it is ready for your projects as the need arises. For example, it is possible to build a web interface to read/write to the GPIO interface of Raspberry Pi (for example, `http://googlecreativelab.github.io/coder-projects/projects/blinky_lights/`).

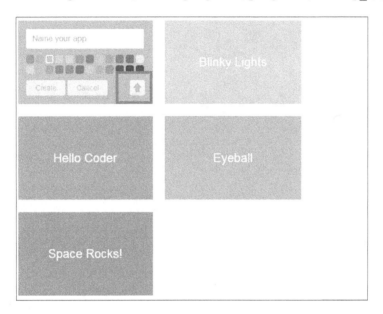

#3 Adafruit Occidentalis

Adafruit Industries released a version of Raspbian, Occidentalis that enabled easier hardware development as it featured drivers for all standard communication protocols. Adafruit Industries also released a web-based development tool that comes with several Python examples.

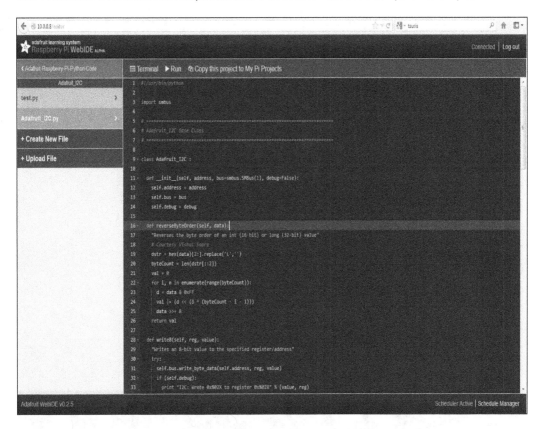

#4 Java Development using the Raspberry Pi

Oracle has released a tutorial set that teaches Java development using Raspberry Pi. This includes tutorials on interface pressure sensors and writing Java code to read barometric pressure data from the sensor via the I2C interface.

#5 The Thingbox project

The ThingBox Project (`http://thethingbox.io/`) is a tool that allows you to enable projects that are related to the Internet of Things on Raspberry Pi. It is a set of tools that allows you to interface sensors and appliances to the Internet, available as an OS image that can be flashed on to an SD card and run on Raspberry Pi. One of the tools available with the ThingBox Project is Node-RED (`http://nodered.org`). The Node-RED tool (shown in following screenshot), in fact, is a graphical interface tool that eliminates the need for you to program to control the devices connected to your Pi. As the name suggests, any application is built using nodes and the control flow is shown by connected wires.

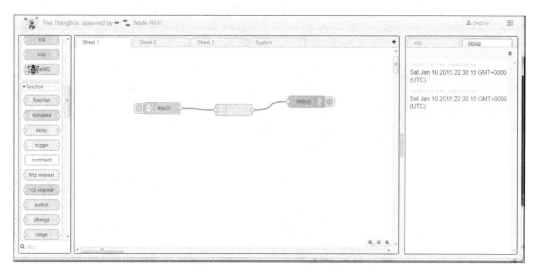

A Hello world project using Node-RED

Remotely logging in the Raspberry Pi from anywhere on the Internet

A company called Weaved (`http://www.weaved.com/`) has released a tool that is still under beta testing while writing this book. It enables you to remotely log in to Raspberry Pi that is connected to the Internet from anywhere on the Web (apart from a local network). There is also a tutorial to install and use the tool (`https://www.juicypi.io/access-your-raspberry-pi-anywhere-in-the-world-using-weaved/`). This enables remote control/data collection.

Problems that might be encountered while using Raspberry Pi

The following are some problems we encountered while we worked on Raspberry Pi.

SD card corruption

We encountered SD card corruptions while working with Raspberry Pi. In some cases, we had to discard the SD card but in other cases, we were able to recover the SD card using **Advanced Partition Scanner Wizard** and re-image the SD card.

Sometimes the failure occurs because there is a power failure while the card is still being written to. Such failures are unavoidable over the life of your projects. Here are a few ways to avoid SD card corruption:

- ▶ Power down your Pi properly after use
- ▶ Charge your battery packs and make sure Pi has a constant power supply at all times

Be sure to buy good quality SD cards and as with everything else digital, have backups.

Power issues

We encountered issues related to the power draw of Raspberry Pi. We had little success with things such as a battery pack (we were able to get it working using a 2700 mAh battery pack). As you may be aware, Raspberry Pi needs a 1 A, 5 V USB power supply.

Devices powered by USB

Some devices such as a webcam cannot be connected directly to the Raspberry Pi and a USB hub may be necessary to connect such devices.

Cool add-on hardware sources developed for the Raspberry Pi platform

There are several products and add-on hardware developed specifically for Raspberry Pi. Most of them are designed specifically for Raspberry Pi. Some of them are available through DIY product sellers such as Sparkfun and Adafruit Industries. Most products are developed through crowdfunding sites such as Kickstarter and Indiegogo. We made our best effort to introduce a new piece of hardware in each project. A simple web search should pop up a new product for a specific application.

The Raspberry Pi model B versus B+, model A versus A+

The Raspberry Pi model A+ and B+ has more GPIO pins than the model A and B. The model B+ has two more USB ports while model A+ consumes less power than the model A. Hence, it is possible use a power over Ethernet module (PoE). Check out `http://www.silvertel.com/component/content/article/22-latest-news/304-raspberry-pi-poe.html` for more information.

If you own a Raspberry Pi B+ but the hardware you own is compatible with Raspberry Pi model B, you can make use of a 40 pin to 26 pin adapter available from Adafruit Industries (`https://www.adafruit.com/products/1986`).

Project ideas that can be implemented over a weekend

Besides what you have seen so far in this book, there are several cool projects that can be implemented in a week or less. These include the following:

- A smart alarm clock based on Raspberry Pi, with features such as custom alarm sounds, period, snooze options, the ability to report weather conditions, alert you about today's to-do list, and much more.
- Home automation and home surveillance systems, a camera that works on motion, VOC alarms, mood lighting, lighting controls, and so on.
- A sensor network, wired or wireless, to monitor various parameters around your house—temperature, plants, pets, and others.
- A digital photo frame network that changes images across many frames, depending on the time of the day and so on.
- Seasonal projects such as lights for Diwali, Hanukah, or Christmas.

Useful resources for the Raspberry Pi

In this section, we will discuss useful resources that are available for Raspberry Pi. While this book can cover every aspect of the projects developed in this book, we will definitely run into trouble. Let's look at some user communities that can try to address our problem.

Raspberry Pi Foundation's forums:

The Raspberry Pi Foundation (http://www.raspberrypi.org/forums/) has maintained a forum since its inception. This forum provides answers to a vast spectrum of questions that you may have. It also offers an opportunity to directly interact with the creators of Raspberry Pi.

Raspberry Pi Stack Exchange:

At the time of writing this book, the Raspberry Pi Stack Exchange (http://raspberrypi.stackexchange.com/) was in the public beta testing mode. If this site passes the beta testing phase, it should also contain a pool of useful resources.

Element 14's Raspberry Pi community:

The Element 14 website (http://www.element14.com/community/community/raspberry-pi) hosts a series of blog posts from Raspberry Pi users who have built an ecosystem of gadgets surrounding Raspberry Pi. The community web page hosts contests regularly in order to exhibit the talent of Raspberry Pi enthusiasts and DIY hobbyists. The community web page also has a user forum to exchange information, ask questions related to order status, and so on.

Mission accomplished

In this project, we discussed certain project ideas, tips, and tricks and problems you might encounter while working on a project using Raspberry Pi. The authors sincerely hope that you have enjoyed this book.

Index

W

Weasley weather clock
  about 54, 55
  assembling 56
  requisites 55
Weaved
  URL 206
web development
  Google Coder used 220
WebIDE. *See* **Raspberry Pi WebIDE**
web.py framework 77
web server
  installing 90, 91
  interfacing 92-95

  setting up, for recording
    health parameters 186-188
Win32DiskImager tool 11
Windows
  SD card with Raspbian image, flashing 11, 12
WinSCP
  URL 217
WonderHowTo
  URL 113
Wordnik API
  installing 208
  URL 208
  using 208, 209
WordOfTheDay object
  URL 209

 **Thank you for buying**
Raspberry Pi Mechatronics Projects HOTSHOT

About Packt Publishing

Packt, pronounced 'packed', published its first book, *Mastering phpMyAdmin for Effective MySQL Management*, in April 2004, and subsequently continued to specialize in publishing highly focused books on specific technologies and solutions.

Our books and publications share the experiences of your fellow IT professionals in adapting and customizing today's systems, applications, and frameworks. Our solution-based books give you the knowledge and power to customize the software and technologies you're using to get the job done. Packt books are more specific and less general than the IT books you have seen in the past. Our unique business model allows us to bring you more focused information, giving you more of what you need to know, and less of what you don't.

Packt is a modern yet unique publishing company that focuses on producing quality, cutting-edge books for communities of developers, administrators, and newbies alike. For more information, please visit our website at www.packtpub.com.

Writing for Packt

We welcome all inquiries from people who are interested in authoring. Book proposals should be sent to author@packtpub.com. If your book idea is still at an early stage and you would like to discuss it first before writing a formal book proposal, then please contact us; one of our commissioning editors will get in touch with you.

We're not just looking for published authors; if you have strong technical skills but no writing experience, our experienced editors can help you develop a writing career, or simply get some additional reward for your expertise.

Raspberry Pi Networking Cookbook

ISBN: 978-1-84969-460-5   Paperback: 204 pages

An epic collection of practical and engaging recipes for the Raspberry Pi!

1. Learn how to install, administer, and maintain your Raspberry Pi.

2. Create a network fileserver for sharing documents, music, and videos.

3. Host a web portal, collaboration wiki, or even your own wireless access point.

4. Connect to your desktop remotely, with minimum hassle.

Raspberry Pi Home Automation with Arduino

ISBN: 978-1-84969-586-2   Paperback: 176 pages

Automate your home with a set of exciting projects for the Raspberry Pi!

1. Learn how to dynamically adjust your living environment with detailed step-by-step examples.

2. Discover how you can utilize the combined power of the Raspberry Pi and Arduino for your own projects.

3. Revolutionize the way you interact with your home on a daily basis.

Please check **www.PacktPub.com** for information on our titles

Raspberry Pi Cookbook for Python Programmers

ISBN: 978-1-84969-662-3   Paperback: 402 pages

Over 50 easy-to-comprehend tailor-made recipes to get the most out of the Raspberry Pi and unleash its huge potential using Python

1. Install your first operating system, share files over the network, and run programs remotely.

2. Unleash the hidden potential of the Raspberry Pi's powerful Video Core IV graphics processor with your own hardware accelerated 3D graphics.

3. Discover how to create your own electronic circuits to interact with the Raspberry Pi.

4. Interface with purpose-built add-ons and adapt off-the-shelf household devices.

Instant Raspberry Pi Gaming

ISBN: 978-1-78328-323-1   Paperback: 60 pages

Your guide to gaming on the Raspberry Pi, from classic arcade games to modern 3D adventures

1. Learn something new in an Instant! A short, fast, focused guide delivering immediate results.

2. Play classic and modern video games on your new Raspberry Pi computer.

3. Learn how to use the Raspberry Pi app store.

4. Written in an easy-to-follow, step-by-step manner that will have you gaming in no time.

Please check **www.PacktPub.com** for information on our titles

www.ingramcontent.com/pod-product-compliance
Lightning Source LLC
LaVergne TN
LVHW062312060326
832902LV00013B/2178